A Shortened Version
of the Bible

Daniel Gwira

Strategic Book Publishing and Rights Co.

A Shortened Version of the Bible © 2012

By Daniel Gwira

Strategic Book Publishing and Rights Co.
12620 FM 1960, Suite A4-507
Houston, TX 77065
www.sbpra.com

ISBN: 978-1-61204-888-8

Design: Dedicated Book Services, Inc. (www.netdbs.com)

Introduction

It's a fact that very few people have actually read the whole Bible. Everybody has read parts of it, and it has proved to be an inspiration to many over the years.

I decided to try to read the Bible once in my life and take notes. It took me almost a year, and I realised that though the Message was clear, powerful and good, most of it, especially the Old Testament, was too long and there was no way I would want to read it twice. The notes I took were so that I would not have to read the whole Bible again, in order to be able to know what it was all about.

Encouraged by The Reverend George Dyke and The Reverend Willie Bridcut, in Ireland, the notes I took finally gave birth to this shortened version of the Bible. I have done my best to promote the aspects that emphasise the greatness of God and the teachings of Jesus Christ and His followers, in a way that makes it easier to read and understand without losing the basic Message and without actually interfering with God's written Word.

This shortened version of the Bible is for all those who for their own reasons have not had the time, the patience, or the will to read the longer version. If after reading this version, one realises that there is only one God whom we must love and His Commandments obey, then this book would have achieved its aim and purpose. It is after all only a shortened version of the Bible and nothing more!

Daniel Gwira (Dublin 1995)

"Daniel Gwira presents in 'A Shortened Version of the Bible', a suitably selected and well-constructed version of the 'Heilgeschichte;' the Salvation Story contained in the collection of sacred writings known as the Bible, from Genesis to the Revelation of St. John. It is carefully and accurately done and reflects great merit on Daniel Gwira. It may

be earnest (sic) of other valuable work in the area. This useful and interesting work is a winner!"
Dr. Donald Caird (Archbishop of Dublin 1998)

"Your book will be a tremendous aid to those who wish to know in brief what the Bible is all about in particular; it will be helpful to those who find the books of the Old Testament a bit confusing and who are wary of approaching the full text. I pray that your 'A Shortened Version of the Bible' will inspire and give confidence to many people to make the study and praying of the Word of God a critical part of their daily lives. Once again, I commend you on the great work you have done in the production of this book."
Archbishop Seán Brady (Archbishop of Armagh and Primate of all Ireland 1998)

Dedicated to Auntie Julie. May she rest in peace.

"Jesus is my protector!"

Table of Contents

THE OLD TESTAMENT

THE BOOK OF GENESIS

God made the heavens and the earth. He divided a day into light and darkness. He created water, vegetation, all living creatures and then made man in His own image to rule over everything. He did all this in six days and rested on the seventh. He blessed the seventh day and made it sacred. He then made the Garden of Eden, which had the very best vegetation and put Adam, the man He had created, in it. He told the man to eat anything he liked except the fruit of the tree of the knowledge of good and evil. He then created a female called Eve as a companion for the man.

One day, the serpent convinced Eve to eat the fruit of the tree, and she gave some to Adam. Their eyes opened, and they realised they were naked. God cursed them and expelled them from the garden.

They had two sons, Cain and Abel. Because God accepted Abel and his offering and rejected Cain and his offering, Cain became angry and killed Abel. When God asked him of Abel's whereabouts, he replied, *"Am I my brother's keeper?"* God expelled him and put a mark on him so that anyone seeing him would not kill him. Cain went to live in Nod, East of Eden, where he had a son called Enoch and built a town also called Enoch after his son, and a family was formed.

God realised that man was becoming evil and regretted making him. Noah, however, found favour with Him. So God told him to build an Ark because He was going to destroy humanity. He was to board the Ark with his family and a pair of all animals and birds in the world. He was to take enough food because God was going to flood the earth. There was a flood that lasted a hundred and fifty days during which everything except the Ark was destroyed. God then blessed Noah and told him to be productive and reproduce in order to increase his family.

At one time, there was only one language, and the people tried to build a tower into Heaven so God confused them by making them speak different languages, and then the Tower of Babel was abandoned.

Out of the descendants of Noah came Abraham, who was the son of Terah and the grandson of Nahor, and Lot. Abraham, his wife, Sarah, and Lot were told by God to leave their land to settle in Bethel. When a famine struck, Abraham went to Egypt and was treated well by Pharaoh because of his interest in Sarah. When he found out that Sarah was his wife, Pharaoh escorted Abraham and all his possessions out of Egypt. Lot settled in the Jordan area. Abraham settled near Hebron and built an altar to God.

Sodom and Gomorrah were defeated by Chedorlaomer, who also captured Lot. On hearing the news, Abraham gathered his army and defeated Chedorlaomer and saved Lot. He returned all the property belonging to the king of Sodom and refused to take a reward.

Abraham had a vision in which God affirmed His faith and support in him. Sarah could not have children, so Abraham had a son called Ishmael with her maid Hagar. God confirmed His Covenant (a promise to love and protect, which elicits the response to obey God's Laws) with Abraham and told him what he should and should not do.

One day two angels saved Lot from the Sodomites who were about to kill him. The angels blinded the men who had come to Lot's house and told him and his family to escape because God was about to destroy the whole place. The angels told them to run to a nearby town, but they were not to look back. God then destroyed Sodom and Gomorrah with sulphur and fire from Heaven. When Lot's wife looked back to see what was happening, she was turned into a pillar of salt.

The town they moved to was called Zoar, but Lot decided to live in a cave nearby with his two daughters who tricked him by getting him drunk and sleeping with him. As a result, they each had a son for him; one was called Moab and became the ancestor of the Moabites, and the other was called Ben Ammi and became the ancestor of the Ammonites.

Abraham moved to the south of the country, and Sarah bore him a son called Isaac. God tested Abraham by asking him to use Isaac as a burnt offering for Him and stopped him at the last minute when he was about to kill Isaac. When Sarah died, Abraham arranged Rebecca as a wife for Isaac through a servant. Isaac married Rebecca, and Abraham also married another wife called Keturah just before he finally died at the age of 175.

Rebecca had two sons, Jacob and Esau. One day, Jacob made Esau sell his birthright for a plate of food when Esau came in from the field longing to eat something. Because of the famine, Isaac kept moving around with his family and settled in Gerar with permission from Abimelech, who was the king there because he knew God was with him.

Jacob stole Esau's blessing from Isaac who was blind and could not recognise Jacob dressed in Esau's clothes. He made out to be Esau who was hairy, by putting skins of hair on the parts of his body (arms and neck) which Isaac might feel and he prepared food for him. When Esau found out, he had a grudge against Jacob. Rebecca told Jacob to run away to her brother Laban at Haran, otherwise Esau would kill him.

Jacob in his travels had a dream in which he recognised the power of God and how it was helping him. On reaching Haran, he worked for seven years for Laban in order to be allowed to marry his daughter Rachel. He was given Leah, his other daughter, instead and had to work for another seven years for Rachel. Jacob eventually had children with both women and their maids. Rachel who was infertile at first eventually bore Joseph and Benjamin.

Jacob got fed up with Laban cheating him and ran away with his family. Laban chased him and caught up with him, but he had a dream in which God persuaded him not to harm Jacob.

Jacob sent cows, goats, and other animals as a peace offering to Esau who helped him settle in Succoth. Jacob's name was changed to Israel by a man with whom he wrestled because Jacob refused to let the man go unless the man blessed him.

When Hamor, a local chief's son raped Dinah (Jacob's daughter by Leah), her brothers went to town and killed every male. God told Jacob to move to Bethel, get rid of all their strange gods, and build an altar to Him. He then confirmed Jacob's name to Israel. Rachel died after giving birth to Benjamin, her second child. Jacob finally settled in Canaan.

Israel loved Joseph more than his other sons. The brothers hated Joseph and plotted against him. They did not like the idea of his dreams or his coat of many colours, so one day they caught him in a field and sold him to the Ishmaelites, much to the horror of Reuben, the only brother who loved him. He found Joseph's coat that had secretly been soaked in goat's blood by his brothers and believed that wild animals had killed him. Israel was told and was greatly bereaved.

One of Israel's grandchildren, called Er (the first born of his son Judah), was such a wicked person in God's presence that God ended his life. The same happened to his brother Onan who refused to sleep with Er's widow Tamar. (He used to spill his sperm on the ground to prevent his brother from having more children.) Tamar then tricked Judah into sleeping with her and conceived the twins, Perez and Zarah.

Joseph was taken to Egypt and Pharaoh's captain bought him from the Ishmaelites to whom he had been sold. Joseph did so well he became the captain's orderly and later his superintendent.

When Joseph refused to sleep with the captain's wife, she seized his coat, accused him of attempted rape, and he was thrown into prison. However, God was with him, and he was entrusted to be in charge of all the convicts in the prison.

Also in the prison were Pharaoh's butler and baker who both dreamed and had Joseph interpret their dreams. Joseph said that within three days Pharaoh would reprieve the butler but hang the baker. When everything happened as he had said, the reprieved butler forgot about Joseph who spent another two years in prison before being asked to interpret Pharaoh's dreams because no one else could. Joseph said that Egypt would have seven years of abundance followed by seven years of famine. He then advised Pharaoh to store food for the famine. Pharaoh was so grateful that he put Joseph in charge of the whole of Egypt. He gave Joseph a ring and married him to a priest's daughter called Asenath. They had two sons called Manasseh and Ephraim.

The famine came and was so severe that people came from different countries to buy grain from Joseph. Jacob sent all his sons except Benjamin to buy grain from Egypt. Joseph accused them of being spies and jailed them for three days. He then gave them food and told them to go home and bring their youngest brother. He kept Simeon as hostage while they went. None of them recognised Joseph. They later found that their money had been returned in the sacks of grain that Joseph had given them, and they were afraid. They returned with Benjamin, and Joseph could no longer control his emotions and revealed himself to them. He forgave them for what they did to him when he discovered that they were changed men. Joseph had tested them to see if they hated Benjamin, his full brother. They returned home and brought Jacob to meet Joseph who introduced them to Pharaoh. Pharaoh allowed them to settle in the choicest part of the land and gave them everything they needed.

The famine was so severe that the people ran out of money and had to trade their livestock and land for food. Only the priests were exempt. Joseph had made Pharaoh very rich as he now owned everything in Egypt. Before Jacob died, he blessed his twelve sons who became the founders of the twelve tribes of Israel. Joseph buried Jacob in Canaan and returned with his brothers to Egypt where he looked after them.

Joseph finally died aged 110 and was buried in Egypt.

THE BOOK OF EXODUS

Jacob's children increased so much they became a threat to the new Pharaoh of Egypt who had no knowledge of what Joseph had done. Although the Egyptians treated the Israelites badly and made them slaves, they continued to multiply.

Pharaoh ordered that every male baby born to the Israelites should be thrown into the Nile River and drowned. A Levite woman hid her baby in a watertight basket and put him into the Nile. Pharaoh's daughter found the basket with the baby floating amongst the reeds, and she paid the child's mother to nurse him. She called him Moses.

Moses grew up very strong, and one day killed an Egyptian who was beating up a Hebrew. Pharaoh found out, and Moses had to run away. He was looked after by Jethro, a Midianite priest who gave him his daughter Zipporah to marry. They had a son called Gershom.

God saw how the Israelites were suffering, and so He spoke to Moses out of a burning bush and told him that he would lead his people out of Egypt to the Promised Land. The bush was on fire but did not burn up. When Moses said that the people would not believe him, God turned his staff into a snake, made his hand leprous, and promised to help him convince his people, just to show him that He indeed had the power.

Moses returned to Egypt with his family. God sent Aaron to meet him in the desert, and they became partners. Moses went to ask Pharaoh to let his people leave Egypt, but Pharaoh refused to listen and ordered his people to make work more difficult for the Israelites, who in any case, found it difficult to believe Moses.

Pharaoh refused to let the Israelites go, even after Aaron's staff had become a snake. Instead, he called his magicians who performed the same trick. Moses and Aaron then turned the river into blood, and the fish died. There was such a stench that no one could drink from it. Pharaoh's magicians did the same. Aaron then stretched his hands over the rivers, and Egypt was covered in frogs. Again, the magicians did the same. When God killed all the frogs for Pharaoh, he almost let the Israelites go, but then changed his mind and refused to let them leave. Aaron then invoked the gnats on the population. This time the magicians failed. Pharaoh, however, again proved stubborn.

God invaded Egypt with gadflies, and Pharaoh agreed to let the people go. As soon as the gadflies left, he changed his mind. The next day all the livestock belonging to the Egyptians died. None belonging to the Israelites was harmed. When Pharaoh again refused, all the Egyptians were covered in sores, and God sent down hail, thunder, and lightning. This did not convince Pharaoh, so God sent locusts to destroy all the crops.

Moses then stretched his hands towards Heaven, and there was darkness over the whole of Egypt for three days. Pharaoh was still not convinced and refused to let them go, even after being threatened that every first born in Egypt was to die. God had given Moses certain rules for his people, which included forbidding them to eat leavened bread (this is bread with a substance that makes it rise, like yeast) for seven days, offering sacrifices to Him, and celebrating with a feast. God had told them that He would lead the Israelites out in a hurry, and so they would have no time to wait for bread to rise.

When God killed every first born, Pharaoh was finally convinced and allowed them to leave. About six hundred thousand Israelites left Egypt, led by Moses and Aaron. They had stayed in Egypt for four hundred and thirty years.

They first moved from Ramesh to Succoth. God told Moses to dedicate every first born in Israel to Him, in order to commemorate their freedom. No leavened bread should be eaten.

The Israelites trekked through the desert by the Red Sea instead of going through Philistine country where there might have been war. Pharaoh gathered his army and chased them, catching up with them at the Red Sea. Moses raised his staff and God divided the sea into two, and the Israelites walked through on dry land. The Egyptians followed and God returned the waters, which drowned the Egyptian army. The Israelites sang praises to God and moved to the Shur Desert.

The people complained of the lack of water to drink and food to eat, which God then miraculously provided. The people called it manna from Heaven. The Israelites ate the manna for forty years until they reached the outskirts of Canaan. God again provided water at the Horeb rock that He asked Moses to strike with his rod. The water came out of it as soon as Moses hit it.

Led by Joshua, the Israelites defeated Amalek and his people, while Moses held his hand in the air. Jethro, Moses' father-in-law, came to him with his wife, Zipporah, and his two sons, Gershom and Eliezar. Moses then began to administer justice to his people and chose able men to be his deputies to help him because of Jethro's advice. Jethro then returned to his country.

God then told Moses to tell his people to obey His Commandments because they were a holy nation. Moses took the people to the base of Mount Sinai. God came down in smoke and fire, met Moses on the mountain, and gave him the Ten Commandments and all the other laws that had to be obeyed. Moses came down and told the people about the two stone tablets with the Commandments written on them. For six days, a cloud covered the mountain, and on the seventh, God called Moses up to the mountain, and he stayed there for forty days and nights. God then told Moses to make an offering and build a Sanctuary to Him; He described in detail how it should be built. God then showed Aaron and Moses how to consecrate everything to Him with burnt offerings and prayers, in order to atone for their sins. God also showed Moses how to build the altar. Every Israelite also had to give a ransom to God during the census so that no plague or misfortune would fall on them as they were being counted.

God told Moses to anoint Aaron and his sons as priests and also to make perfumes that should be dedicated to Him. The Sabbath was to be kept sacred, and anyone who profaned it would be eliminated.

Because Moses had taken so long coming down from the mountain, the Israelites complained to Aaron to find them other gods. Aaron told them to bring him all their gold, and he had it moulded into a golden calf. He then built an altar and proclaimed a feast to God. God was angry and wanted to destroy them, but Moses pleaded with Him to forgive them.

Moses finally came down from the mountain with the two tablets that had God's Commandments written on them. He was angry with Aaron when he saw the people rejoicing and broke the two tablets. He told the Levites to each kill his brother. About three thousand were killed.

Moses went back up the mountain and asked God to forgive them. God said that He would punish them in due course. God made another two stone tablets for Moses who bowed and worshipped Him. God made a Covenant with him to protect them, but they had to obey His Commandments. He then gave Moses a set of rules for them to obey, which were basically:

1. They were to have no other gods except the one true God who brought them out of slavery.
2. This one true God was to be worshipped in a proper way. No idols or images were to be used. Images are easily turned into other gods, and God is a jealous God who will not tolerate any rival and will punish up till the third and fourth generations of those who hate Him. He will, however, show kindness to those who love Him and obey His Commandments.
3. They should not abuse His Name or use it profanely. Those who did that would not be regarded as innocent.
4. They should observe the Sabbath as a holy day and do all their work on the other six days in the week. Not even servants or animals should do any work on the Sabbath.

   5. All should honour and respect their parents.
   6. They should not kill.
   7. They should not commit adultery.
   8. They should not steal.
   9. They should not tell lies or give false witness to or for any-body.
   10. They should not have any designs on each others' wives, husbands, servants, animals or anything else that does not belong to them. These later became known as the *Ten Commandments*.

Moses returned from the mountain with his face glowing, and the people were afraid of him. He got all the Israelites together and told them what they had to do. They all brought their contributions for the construction of the Tabernacle. God gave them all the necessary skills needed to build the Tabernacle, which was soon completed according to God's directions to Moses. Moses then anointed it with oil, deposited the Testimony inside the Ark, and brought the Ark inside the Tabernacle. God covered it with a cloud by day and fire by night, and the people could travel only when the cloud was lifted.

THE BOOK OF LEVITICUS

In this book God states all His rules concerning offerings, sacrifices, and life in general. God also states the duties of priests and Levites. The book emphasises the holiness of God and the need to approach Him in the proper way.

God told Moses and Aaron to explain to the Israelites the penalties for sinning against Him and what should be done to atone for the sins. The atonement for sins involved the sacrifice of clean and pure livestock, burnt offerings, and food offerings.

Moses and Aaron then gave up two rams and a calf to God, in order to atone for all the sins of the people. They killed the animals as a burnt offering to God. When Nadab and Abihu, the sons of Aaron, went about a burnt offering the wrong way, they were killed by God.

God explained to Moses which animals and birds one could and could not eat and what to do about sores, spots, burns, and other diseases to the human body in general. The emphasis was on cleanliness and how the unclean should be separated from the clean and what to do to become clean again after a disease. This involved the sacrifice of birds as sin and burnt offerings.

God told Moses to tell Aaron not to enter the holy place where the Ark was or he would die like his sons, unless he first offered a bullock and a ram as sin and burnt offerings. Any animal that was butchered had first to be offered as a gift to God. Any person who did not do that would die. Nobody should eat the blood of any animal.

God also gave the rules concerning sex with close relatives. Homosexuality and incest were wrong, so was bestiality. Those who broke the rules would die. All offerings to God had to be pleasing to Him. There should be no other gods except for Him and no idols. One had to be just in a court of law, but above all one should love his neighbour.

Anybody who killed should be killed; an eye for an eye and a tooth for a tooth. The son of an Israelite woman and an Egyptian man were stoned to death for blaspheming God's Name.

God stated the laws for property, making them aware that all land belonged to Him, and so one should not sell for a profit, and one should always help an impoverished brother or neighbour. If they obeyed God's Laws and had no other gods apart from Him, then He would make sure that they always prospered. He would make them safe from enemies, wild beasts, and the elements. Food would always be in abundance. If, however, they did not listen to or revere Him, then terror, sickness, and bad harvests would always trouble them followed by terrible plagues and death. Life would not be worth living, even for the survivors.

All land should become free of ownership after fifty years and should be returned to the original owner. On a special year that was called the Jubilee, all slaves were to be freed, and all land was to lay fallow for that year.

THE BOOK OF NUMBERS

God told Moses to take a census of all the Israelites according to their families and clans. Every male over twenty years of age would be conscripted into their respective armies. The leader of each tribe was to help him, and 603,550 were subject to military service. The Levites were not included in the census. They were to be put in charge of the Tabernacle. The armies were then given their respective jobs to protect the people. Those who were not clean, like the lepers, those who had emissions or those who had touched a corpse, were to be sent outside the camp to live. Any woman who committed adultery with or without the husband's knowledge would be cursed. Those wanting to live in consecration to God had to abstain from wine, intoxicants, shaving, or going near a corpse. This was called taking the vow of the Nazarite.

After Moses had finished setting up the Tabernacle, the princes of Israel and leaders of the tribal houses brought gifts of wagons and livestock to the Lord, which were given to the Levites to help them in their work. The princes then gave other gifts for the altar, mostly of gold and silver.

God instructed Moses to tell the Israelites to observe the Passover and to blow trumpets to signal the summoning and breaking of camp. The Israelites travelled for three days to a new site, preceded by the Tabernacle. When some people came to complain to Moses about their misfortunes, God heard them and killed some of them with fire until Moses begged Him to stop. The place where this happened was called Taberah. The people kept complaining about not having meat to eat and that they were better off in Egypt. God sent so many quails down to them that they spent two days trying to pick them up. God then struck them with the plague, and many people died. This was at Kibroth-hattaavah.

The people then moved camp to Hazeroth, where they remained. When Miriam complained about Moses marrying a

Cushite woman, God got angry and turned her into a leper. Aaron pleaded for her, and God reinstated her only after she had spent seven days excluded from the camp.

The people again moved camp to the wilderness of Paran. Moses sent Caleb and some spies to check out the land of Canaan. They returned after forty days claiming that the land was flowing with milk and honey, but that the people living there were strong and their cities fortified.

The people again started complaining to Moses and Aaron and even suggested going back to Egypt. Joshua tried to appease them by saying that they would conquer the new land because God was with them. The crowd were on the verge of stoning Moses, Aaron, and Joshua, when God appeared to the whole nation. He threatened to destroy them with the plague, but once again relented when Moses interceded on their behalf. God promised that none of those who had grumbled against Him would ever see the Promised Land and their corpses would rot in the wilderness. Only Joshua and Caleb who had a different attitude would survive and enter the Promised Land. After rotting in the wilderness, their children would suffer a further forty years wandering as shepherds in the desert. The spies who had started a whispering campaign against God were killed by a plague. God then told Moses to tell the people to offer burnt offerings to Him as soon as they arrived in the Promised Land.

When a man was caught gathering wood on the Sabbath, God directed that he be stoned to death. Korath, Datham, and Abiram revolted against the authority of Moses and Aaron and tried to get the people to go against them. The earth opened up and swallowed them, their families, and their property. A fire then killed 250 more of their followers. The people again complained, and 14,700 more were killed by a plague sent by God. God then gave them rules for the presentation of offerings and gifts. Anyone who desecrated the holy gifts of the Israelites would die.

When the people arrived at Zin, which was in the wilderness, they stayed in Kadesh where Miriam died and was buried. Moses struck a rock with his rod, and water came gushing out. This was after the Israelites had again complained about having nothing to drink. Because Moses and Aaron did not trust in God enough to vindicate Him in the eyes of the people, they were told that they would never see the Promised Land.

When Moses sent a message to the king of Edom for permission to pass through his land, he refused and threatened to attack them. So they left Kadesh and went to Mount Hor where Aaron died and his robes were passed on to his son Eliezar.

The king of Arad a Canaanite, attacked the Israelites and took some of them prisoner, but the Israelites prayed, and they destroyed the Canaanites in another battle at Hormah. When the Israelites again complained about food and water, God sent snakes amongst them, and many of them died. God only stopped when Moses interceded on their behalf.

They continued on their travels, and when Sihon, the king of the Amorites, refused them entry through his country and attacked them, he was soundly defeated, and the Israelites seized all his cities and settled in them. They then destroyed Og, the king of Bashan.

The Israelites continued on their travels and set up camp in the plains of Moab. Balak, the son of Zippor the king of Moab, tried to solicit Balaam to attack the Israelites, but Balaam was restrained by God.

When the Israelites started having illicit relations with the Moab women and worshipping their gods, Moses executed the ring leaders, and 24,000 of them died of the plague. Zimri, an Israelite, was found with Cozbi, a Midianite woman, and both were killed by Phinehas, the son of Eliezar and grandson of Aaron.

God told Moses to take a new census after the plague, putting those over twenty years of age into military service. Each tribe was allotted its inheritance of the land. When the daughters of Zelophehad, who were descendants of Manasseh, complained about being left out of the inheritance because they were women, God told Moses to give them their just share.

God then showed Moses the Promised Land but told him he would not live to see it because he failed to vindicate Him in front of the Israelites. He told Moses to appoint Joshua as his heir in front of the people. He then told Moses to show the people how to go about the offerings to Him on the Sabbath, Passover, the beginning of each month, and during festivals. The husband was confirmed as having authority over his wife in marriage, divorce, and sacred vows.

Moses then raised an army and defeated the Midianites, capturing their women, children, and property. They killed every male. But Moses got angry and told them to kill every male boy and every female who was not a virgin. Moses then taxed the soldiers who had been in battle as a contribution to God. They gave mostly jewellery, gold, and silver. All the tribes were allotted land. God then told Moses to drive out all the natives from Canaan as soon as they crossed the river Jordan and to smash all their images, idols, and false gods. Property was to be shared according to the size of the family. The Levites were to be given special towns to live in. All manslayers would be sent to suitable towns for their own protection. All murderers would be executed. Other laws concerning marriage, property, and inheritance were explained by God to Moses.

THE BOOK OF
DEUTERONOMY

Moses summarized their journey to the people of Israel as they reached the Promised Land, stressing what they went through and how God helped them to reach where they were, with all the miracles and saving them from their enemies. Moses then chastised them for not having complete faith in God and repeated all the things that they should and should not do concerning their offerings, sacrifices, idols, images, crime, sharing of property, sex, adultery, marriage, and life in general. He also told them what punishments would hit those who disobeyed God's Laws and what calamities they would face if they continued to go against Him. In the end, Moses told them to love each other but above all to love and obey God and everything would go well with them in the land of milk and honey, free from enemies, plagues, hunger, sickness, wild animals, and calamities. The other alternative would be plunder, destruction, and death from their enemies.

One day, God appeared in a cloud at the tent of meeting, and Moses confirmed Joshua as his successor. He then sang a song in praise of God, after God had told him that after his death, the people would revert to their old sinful ways and He would abandon them and destroy them.

Moses then blessed the twelve tribes of Israel and went up from the plains of Moab to Mount Nebo, to the top of Pisgah (opposite Jericho). God showed him the whole of the Promised Land that he was not going to be allowed to enter because he had not shown enough faith by not vindicating Him to the grumbling Israelites during the journey.

Moses was 120 years old when he died. Joshua's spirit became filled with wisdom, and he took over. The people listened to him because that was what God wanted. Since then, there has never been a prophet equal to Moses who actually knew God face to face.

THE BOOK OF JOSHUA

God told Joshua to take the Israelites across the Jordan River to the Promised Land. He told them to keep practising the Law and that He would never fail them.

Joshua sent two men to spy on Jericho; they were helped by a harlot called Rahab who hid them in her house when the king of Jericho found out about them. She helped them to escape and asked them to spare her and her family when they returned. She promised not to give them away. They returned to Joshua to tell him that it was safe to cross.

Joshua told the priests to carry the Ark ahead of the people, and they all crossed the Jordan River that God had parted so that they walked on dry land. Joshua told the priests to pick up twelve stones (representing the tribes of Israel) from the river bottom and bring them to serve as a memorial. As soon as they had crossed, the waters of the Jordan returned to its place.

Joshua then circumcised all the Israelites, and they survived on the crops of the land as there was no manna for them. Joshua had a vision of God, who told him to remove his shoes as he was standing on holy land. The priests carried the Ark as they surrounded the city of Jericho. Joshua's army attacked and destroyed the city, killing everybody and everything except for Rahab and her family who had helped the two spies.

Joshua tried to attack Ai but was repulsed and lost thirty-six men, because Achan had stolen something from Jericho during the invasion. Joshua tore his clothes and prayed to God who told him that they had sinned. Achan confessed to having stolen some gold, silver, and a robe. Joshua had him, all his family, and his property stoned and cremated. The place that this happened was called the valley of Achor.

Joshua sent thirty thousand men to attack Ai. Five thousand were used as a decoy to draw away the troops from Ai who pursued them, leaving their city and Bethel unguarded and open for Joshua to go in and burn them to the ground. They then destroyed the troops and captured the king of Ai who was hanged and buried under a pile of stones. Joshua built an altar for God at Mount Ebal and made an offering and sacrifice of thanksgiving. He then read his people the Law and told them to follow it.

Peace was made with the inhabitants of Gibeon, but the five kings of Jerusalem, Hebron, Jarmuth, Lachish, and Eglon, united against Joshua. Joshua saved the cities of Gibeon, Chephirah, Beeroth, and Kiriath-jearim, making the people work for the Israelites. He then defeated and destroyed the armies of the five kings, helped by God who sent hailstones on to them. The five kings escaped and hid in a cave. Joshua captured them, killed them, and hanged them. He then threw their bodies into a cave. Joshua destroyed Makkedah on the same day.

Libnah, Lachish, Eghon, Hebron, Debir, and the whole country were attacked by Joshua and destroyed, and no one was spared. He then returned to camp at Gilgal. Jabin, king of Hazor, organised the kings of Madon, Shimron, Achshaph, and all the other armies to fight the Israelites, but Joshua destroyed all of them and took all their property. No one was spared. He had now conquered the whole area.

When Joshua had become old, God told him to distribute all the land amongst the tribes. Three tribes, the Reubenites, Manasseh, and Gadites, had already been allotted land by Moses. Moses, however, had not given anything to the Levites because he had told them that God was their heritage.

Joshua blessed Caleb and gave him Hebron as his heritage. Caleb gave his daughter Achsah to Othniel for capturing Kiriathsepher. All the land was shared amongst the tribes, and God blessed them. There were some complaints, but Joshua managed to settle everyone and make them happy by casting lots and distributing the land amongst them. God told Joshua to set aside cities of refuge for manslayers who killed accidentally. They could stay there until their trial or until the death of the chief priest and then they would be free to return to their cities. The Levites were also granted cities to live in as God had commanded through Moses. The cities were all within the holdings of the Israelites. There were forty-eight in number.

Joshua then warned everybody to obey God's Commandments because of His love for them. What is more, He had fulfilled His promise of a homeland. They should love God and walk in His ways. When the Reubenites, the Gadites, and the half tribe of Manasseh built an altar, all the other tribes complained. They defended themselves by saying that they had built it in appreciation to God. Phinehas, son of Eleazar the priest, agreed, and they named the altar, "*A witness between us that the Lord is God.*"

God gave the Israelites peace with all her enemies. Joshua told them that God would always protect them if they obeyed His Laws and did not turn to other gods. If they did turn to other gods, then God would be angry, and they would die and lose everything. The people professed that they would revere God and never go against Him. Joshua wrote all the laws into a large book and left a large stone beneath a sacred tree as a testimony to God.

Joshua died at the age of 110 and was buried in Timnath-serah. Eleazar, the son of Aaron, also died and was buried in Ephraim.

THE BOOK OF JUDGES

God put Judah in charge of the Israelites, and Simeon became the second in command. They defeated the Canaanites, and Jerusalem was destroyed. Caleb gave his daughter
Achsah in marriage to Othniel (the son of Caleb's younger
brother Kenaz) for capturing the town of Kiriath-sepher.
The new generation of Israelites were unfaithful to God,
worshipping other gods, so they were defeated by the king of
Mesopotamia and had to serve him for eight years. Othniel,
the new saviour, delivered them, and they enjoyed peace for
forty years until his death.
The Israelites went back to their ungodly ways so they
were again defeated, this time by the king of Moab, and had
to serve him for eighteen years until God gave them another
chance with a saviour called Ehud, who killed the king of
Moab and defeated his army. Peace was enjoyed for eighty
years.
After the death of Ehud, the Israelites reverted to their
evil ways and were defeated by Jabin the king of Canaan
who oppressed them for twenty years. Barak, the new leader,
destroyed Jabin and his hated army captain Sisera who was
killed by Jael (Heber the Kenite's wife), when she nailed a
peg into his temple while he slept.
When Barak died, Israel reverted to her ungodly ways,
and they were defeated by the Midianites and made to serve
them for seven years. Gideon was made the new leader by
God. He destroyed the Midianites and killed their leaders,
Zebah and Zalmunnah. Israel enjoyed peace for forty years
until the death of Gideon.
Abimelech killed his seventy brothers and took over, as
Israel reverted to her ungodly ways. After three years of mis-
rule, Abimelech was killed. Tola then ruled for twenty-three
years in peace. After his death, Israel went back to doing
what God considered to be evil, so the Philistines and Am-

monites took over and oppressed Israel. Jephthah took over for six years and defeated them.

Israel then enjoyed peace through the reigns of a succession of kings: Ibzan (seven years), Elon (ten years) and Abdon (eight years).

Israel went back to her evil ways and was taken over by the Philistines for forty years. Samson was the Israelite leader for twenty of that period. He was captured by the Philistines because he had confided in Delilah the secret of his strength being in his hair. He was blinded, and later he knocked down the pillars of the building, killing himself and over three thousand Philistines.

There was a period of anarchy when the Israelites destroyed the Benjamites because of the rape and murder of one of their women. They then killed all the men from the town of Jabesh-gilead and gave four hundred virgin women to the few remaining Benjamites in order not to destroy the tribe.

THE BOOK OF RUTH

This is the story of Naomi whose husband and two sons died leaving their wives, Ruth and Orpah, with her. Orpah returned to her family, and Ruth followed her mother-in-law to Bethlehem from Moab.

Ruth worked in a field belonging to Boaz who took her under his wing because the story of her courage in following her mother-in-law was well known and admired. Boaz eventually bought everything that belonged to Elimelech (Naomi's husband) and sons (Chilion and Mahlon) from Naomi and acquired Ruth who had proved to be virtuous and hardworking. He then married her, and she bore him a son who was called Obed, the grandfather of the future king David.

THE FIRST BOOK
OF SAMUEL

Samuel, the son of the formerly childless Hannah and El-kanah, was born and presented as an offering of thanks to God. When he matured, he was chosen by God as His prophet to lead the Israelites.

The Philistines defeated Israel and captured the Ark of God. Eli the priest, who was a leader (judge) in Israel for forty years, died when he heard that his two rascal sons, Hophni and Phinehas, had been killed. God put a curse of haemorrhoids on the Philistines for seven months until they had to return the Ark to the Israelites, with peace offerings to God. On Samuel's recommendation, the Israelites got rid of all their gods and asked God for forgiveness. They then attacked the Philistines and defeated them.

As Samuel got older, the Israelites looked for a new leader, and with God's help, Saul was chosen. He defeated the Ammonites. He and his son Jonathan led the Israelites to defeat the Philistines. Saul then defeated the Amaleks, captured Agag who was their king, and looted the best of their cattle and property against the wishes of God. Samuel got annoyed, gave up on Saul, and killed Agag himself. God rejected Saul from being the king because of this. David was secretly chosen instead.

One day David killed the giant Goliath with a sling shot to his head, and the Philistines were defeated. Saul made David his right arm man and gave him his daughter Michal as his wife. David continued to defeat the Philistines in different battles and became more famous than Saul, who thereby became jealous and angry. He plotted to kill David, but David was warned by his bosom friend, Jonathan, and was able to escape.

David defeated the Philistines in another battle without Saul, after he had heard that Saul had attacked Nob (a town set up for priests) and had killed all of them. Saul chased David to try and kill him, and even gave Michal away to another husband. In the end, David could have killed Saul but did not, cutting off Saul's coat tails instead. Saul in gratitude gave up his vendetta on David. Samuel died, and the whole of Israel was in mourning.

David took Abigail as a wife when her husband Nabal, a drunk, uncouth, and rich miser, died of stroke. David had previously almost killed him when Abigail intervened. This was because he had refused to give some of his sheep to David's men despite the fact that David had protected him from harm during the battles. David also married Ahinoam of Jezreel.

David once again embarrassed Saul by sneaking into his camp and stealing his spear but refusing to kill him. He returned the spear via an intermediary and escaped to live in Philistine country. When Saul heard this, he gave up chasing David.

David lived under the care of Achish, the Philistine leader, raiding certain towns and bringing the loot back to Achish who made him his bodyguard.

As the Philistines prepared for war with the Israelites, David was forced to leave Achish and go back to his town Ziklag, only to find that it had been attacked by the Amalekites and all the women, including his wives, had been captured. David attacked them and rescued the women.

Meanwhile the Philistines defeated the Israelites and killed Jonathan and his brothers. Saul, however, committed suicide.

THE SECOND BOOK
OF SAMUEL

David became the new leader of Judah, while Saul's son Ishboshet became king of Israel. They fought a battle that David won, and he therefore became the overall king. Ishboshet was murdered, and David killed Rechab and Bannah, his murderers.

David then captured Jerusalem and named it the City of David. He finally defeated the Philistines in several battles, and all Israel rejoiced. David took many wives and concubines and had many children. He captured the Ark of God back from the Philistines and took back his wife Michal from her new husband.

After several battles, David and his commander Joab defeated all their opponents, and he became the undisputed leader in Israel. He then defeated the Syrians and the Ammonites.

David made Bathsheba pregnant and then put her husband Uriah on the front line in one of the battles so that he would be killed. When this happened, David married Bathsheba. Her first child died because God did not like what David had done to get her. God sent Nathan the prophet to warn David with the story of a rich man who took a poor man's beloved lamb to prepare as a feast for a guest even though he had huge flocks and herds of his own. David reacted angrily saying that the rich man deserved to die. When, however, he realised that Nathan was talking about him, David accepted that he had done wrong. He fasted, prayed, and was forgiven by God. Bathsheba finally bore him a son, the future king Solomon.

One day, David's son Absalom killed his brother Amnon for raping their sister Tamar. He had to go into hiding for three years before Joab pleaded for him to return and be for-given by David.

Absalom started a revolt against David who had to flee to Jerusalem. The revolt failed, and Joab was forced to kill Absalom. David returned to Jerusalem but was saddened by the death of his son. Joab captured all the people who went against David and killed Amassa, their ring leader. Sheba, who also tried to stir up trouble, was killed by the people he was hiding with, and his head was thrown over the wall to Joab.

There was a three-year famine in Israel caused by Saul's wickedness to the people of Gibeon. David handed over seven of Saul's sons to them, and they were killed. Their bodies were thrown on the hill for God to see. The famine ended with rain after David had collected all the bodies and buried them with Saul's and Jonathan's remains.

David defeated the Philistines in a few more battles. A census conducted by Joab revealed Israel's population to be 800,000 and that of Judah to be 500,000. A fatal plague hit Israel and killed 70,000. David, in despair, built an altar to God who stopped the plague.

THE FIRST BOOK OF KINGS

David made Solomon the new king before he died. Benaiah, Solomon's new right arm man, killed Adonijah who had tried to become king, and Joab, David's general who had supported Adonijah in his bid and became the new general. Solomon was firmly established and married the daughter of the pharaoh of Egypt.

He was then granted his wish of ultimate wisdom from God. After deliberating on two women fighting over a baby, his fame spread. (The real mother was found when he ordered the baby to be cut into two. She was the one who reacted by crying and saying that it should not be killed but rather handed over to the other woman.)

Solomon wrote 3000 proverbs, 1005 songs, and was an expert in every subject. He was at peace with everyone and built a house for God (the Temple), which took seven years to finish. He then brought Hiram, a skilled craftsman from Tyre to work at the buildings, including his own house that took thirteen years to complete. He put all David's treasures into the Temple, including the Ark of God. He also built a fleet at Ezion-geber on the Red Sea then prayed with the whole of Israel, thanking God. A huge congregation came, and he held a feast for seven days, giving offerings to God.

He was also visited by the queen of Sheba, who came with many gifts to listen to his wisdom before she returned to her own country. He built himself an ivory throne and became the richest and wisest king in the world. He had 700 wives and 300 concubines who corrupted his mind to other gods, so God became angry with him and told him that on his death Israel would be divided into two, with ten of the twelve tribes following Jeroboam. Solomon tried to kill

Jeroboam who fled to Shishak, the king of Egypt. Solomon finally died, and his son Rehoboam was made king.

Jeroboam returned from Egypt to confront Rehoboam. A coup forced Rehoboam to escape to Jerusalem, and Jeroboam took over Israel. Only the tribe of Judah remained with Rehoboam.

Jeroboam did many evil things, so Shishak, the Egyptian king, attacked Jerusalem and plundered it. Jeroboam ruled for seventeen years and died. The continuous wars between Jeroboam and Rehoboam are told in more detail in the books of chronicles of the kings of Judah. (The national archives of Judah.)

After the death of Rehoboam, his son Abijah became king of Judah, living in Jerusalem for three years before he died. He was always at war with Jeroboam. He also went against God.

He was followed by Asa who reigned for forty-one years. He was at war with Baasha, the king of Israel, who had followed Nadab, the son of Jeroboam. Asa made God happy.

Baasha killed Nadab after only two years, in order to get to the throne, then killed off the whole house of Jeroboam. He was followed by his son Elah, who ruled Israel for only two years because his captain, Zimri, killed him and took his place. Zimri killed off the whole house of Baasha. He only ruled for seven days and was killed by Omri, his army captain, who took over.

Israel was now divided into two, half following Omri and the other half with Tibni. Omri won, and Tibni died. He ruled for six years doing evil in God's eyes. He was followed by his son Ahab who was the worst evil doer out of all of them, ruling for twenty-two years, following and worshipping the satanic god Baal.

Elijah appeared around this time and was told by God to go and hide by the river Cherith, where he was looked after by a widow. He even saved her son, who was ill, by praying to God.

Elijah met Ahab, who arranged for him to talk to the Is-raelites for deserting God. He dared them to see if their god Baal could make a fire on the altar. Nothing happened, so Elijah then asked God for fire, and it came upon the altar even though it was surrounded by water. The Israelites now believed in God and slaughtered all the prophets of Baal. Ahab ran away to his wife Jezebel who ordered Elijah's death after hearing what had happened.

Elijah escaped to the desert and travelled for forty days and nights until he reached Horeb, the mountain of God, where he lived in a cave and was fed by an angel. After a wind, earthquake, and fire, there was calm, and God told Elijah to go to Damascus and anoint Hazael as king of Syria, Jehu as king of Israel, and Elisha as prophet in his place. He met Elisha first, who followed him and became his servant.

God allowed Ahab to defeat Ben-Hadad, the Syrian king, to prove to him that He was the Lord. Ahab, however, spared Ben-Haddad and returned the captured cities to him.

Meanwhile, Jezebel had a certain man called Naboth stoned for refusing to sell his vineyard to her husband Ahab. Elijah confronted Ahab over Naboth's death, and he re-pented, fasted, tore his clothes, and wore a sackcloth, so God spared him.

Jehoshaphat, son of Asa and the new king of Judah, joined forces with Ahab to attack the Syrians, but Ahab was killed, and his son Ahaziah became king for two years. He was fol-lowed by his son Jehoram who became the king of Israel. Jehoshaphat ruled Judah for twenty-five years before he died.

THE SECOND BOOK
OF KINGS

Ahaziah had fallen ill and died because he did not pray to God. Elijah was taken up to Heaven by chariots and horses, and his coat fell down to Elisha who became the new prophet. Jehoram ruled Israel for twelve years, doing evil in God's eyes. Jehoshaphat and Jehoram consulted with Elisha in order to defeat the rebelling king of Moab.

Elisha raised a woman's son from the dead, helped a woman who was in debt by making oil for her to sell, and then fed over a hundred men with just twenty little loaves and some fruit, with God's help. He then cleansed the Syrian army captain Naaman from his leprosy by telling him to wash seven times in the Jordan River.

When Elisha's servant Gehazi conned money from Naaman because of his cure, money that Elisha himself had refused, Elisha found out, and Gehazi became a leper instead. Elisha then stopped the Syrian army from attacking Israel by making them blind, restoring their sight, giving them a feast, and sending them back home.

Ben-Hadad besieged Samaria and caused a famine, but God made the Syrians run and leave their camp because they heard the sound of horses and chariots of a great army coming. The Israelites then came to the camp and took all the food and property.

There was a famine for seven years, after which Elisha went to Damascus. Ben-Hadad was ill and sent his son Hazael with gifts to Elisha in order to ask him whether he would recover from his illness or not. Elisha said that he would be all right, but God had told him that his father would die. Elisha then started crying because he knew what calamities and disasters that Hazael would bring on to Israel.

The next day, Ben-Hadad was suffocated by Hazael, who became the new king of Syria.

During Joram's (son of Ahab) reign in Israel, Jehoram became king of Judah and ruled for eight years. Even though he did bad things, God did not want to destroy him because of a promise to David to make him and his sons a perpetual light.

Around this time, Edom rebelled against Judah and gave themselves a new king. They were, however, destroyed by Joram. (The rest of what Joram did is written in the national archives of Judah.)

In the twelfth year of Joram's reign, Ahaziah, the son of Jehoram, became king of Judah and only ruled for one year in Jerusalem, doing evil things. He accompanied Joram to war against the Syrians. Joram was wounded and went to Jezreel to recover. Ahaziah went to visit him there.

Meanwhile Elisha told one of the sons of the prophets to go to Ramoth-gilead and anoint Jehu (son of Jehoshaphat) as the new king of Israel. Jehu immediately went to war with Joram. Ahaziah and Jehoram were both killed by Jehu and his men, who later killed Jezebel whose corpse was eaten by dogs. All of Ahab's seventy sons were also killed by Jehu's men. Jehu ruled Israel at Samaria for twenty-eight years before he died. Jehoahaz, his son, then became king.

Hazael defeated the Israelites, who began to lose all their territory. Jehoash became king of Judah at the age of seven. He had been hidden by Jehosheba (Ahaziah's sister) when Jehu's men killed her brother's household. Jehoida the priest ordained him king and destroyed all those who believed in the Baal religion. Jehoida instructed King Jehoash to do what was right in God's eyes, and he ruled for forty years in Jerusalem. He was killed in a palace coup by servants after he had given all the valuables in the Lord's house to Hazael the king of Syria, in order not to be attacked by him. He was followed by his son Amaziah, who became king.

In Israel, Jehu's son Jehoahaz became king after his father died and did evil in God's eyes so God constantly made Syria attack Israel until they hardly had any army left. When he died, his son Joash became king of Israel and ruled for sixteen years, doing evil things.

When Elisha was ill, Joash, the king of Israel, went to see him and started crying that he was being attacked from all sides. Elisha gave him a bow and some arrows and told him to shoot out of the window towards the east. Joash did as he was told. Elisha then said that these were the arrows of victory and asked him to strike the ground with them. Joash did so three times, which made Elisha unhappy because it meant that he would only destroy Syria three times. He had expected Joash to strike the ground five or six times. Elisha died and was buried. At one point, a dead man was brought to life after being put into Elisha's grave.

Israel defeated Judah in a battle, and Amaziah was captured. Joash, the king of Israel, went to Jerusalem and broke down the wall, taking all the gold and silver. Amaziah died, and his son Azariah (Uzziah) became the king of Judah at the age of sixteen.

Jeroboam became king of Israel after the death of his father Joash. When he died, he was followed by his son Zechariah.

A succession of kings came to Judah and Israel, out of which none did right in God's eyes. As a result, Israel was plunged into turmoil regularly plundered by the Syrians.

Azariah did some good things but failed to remove the idols and to stop his people worshipping false gods. God struck him with leprosy, and he died. During Azariah's reign, Zechariah ruled Israel for only six months, doing evil things in God's eyes, just like his fathers. He was cut down at Ibleam by Shallum, who became king in his place. He, however, ruled for only a month and was murdered by Menahem, who took over as king.

Menahem destroyed Tiphsah and her surrounding territories, murdering all the pregnant women. He ruled for ten years doing many evil things. He even bribed Pul, the king of Assyria, with silver to gain his support in holding on to his kingdom.

He was followed by his son Pekahiah who ruled for two years doing evil. Pekah, the son of one of his officials, conspired against him, killed him, and became king in his place. He continued in the evil tradition of his predecessors and was plundered by the king of Assyria who took over some of his cities and carried the inhabitants off to Assyria. Hoshea made a conspiracy against him, killed him, and took over as king.

By this time, Jotham, the son of Azariah (Uzziah), had taken over from his father in Judah. He, like his father, did many good things in God's eyes. Although he constructed the upper gate of God's house, that did not stop the people from worshipping idols and false gods, so God began sending Rezin, the king of Syria, and Pekah, the king of Judah, against them. Jotham died and was replaced by his son Ahaz.

Ahaz continued in the evil tradition and even worshipped idols and false gods himself. He was attacked by Rezin and Pekah but could not be subdued. Rezin, however, managed to regain the town of Elath for the Edomites. Ahaz sent silver and gold to the king of Assyria, who attacked Rezin and killed him. Ahaz then messed up God's house because of Tiglath-pileser, the king of Assyria. He finally died, and his son Hezekiah became king.

Meanwhile Hoshea was doing evil things in Israel. When Shalmaneser came up against him, he became the Assyrian king's servant and paid tribute to him. Shalmaneser found out that he was plotting against him and attacked him, taking over Samaria after laying it under siege for three years. He annexed Israel and incorporated her cities into Assyria.

All this happened because the Israelites had sinned against God after all He had done for them by bringing them out of Egypt. They kept on worshipping false gods and idols. God had on numerous occasions warned them, but they did not listen. The king of Assyria then sent a priest to the annexed cities to teach them right from wrong, but they continued in their evil ways and refused to worship God.

During that time, Hezekiah became king of Judah. Sennacherib, the new king of Assyria, attacked Judah and captured it. Hezekiah was forced to pay a huge ransom and gave away parts of the Lord's house to the king of Assyria. They were so demoralized that Hezekiah, who believed in God, tore his clothes, put on sackcloth, and prayed for the Assyrians to be defeated.

He then sent Eliakim, his messenger, to Isaiah with his problem. Isaiah told him that he should not worry but God had heard him and He would destroy the Assyrians for him. That night God killed 185,000 Assyrians, and they were forced to leave the captured lands. Sennacherib himself was killed by his own sons, and one of them, Esar-haddon, became the new king of Assyria.

Hezekiah became ill and was visited by Isaiah, who advised him to pray to God. God decided to add fifteen years to his life so that he might be able to witness the defeat of the Assyrians. Hezekiah finally died and was followed by his son Manasseh.

Manasseh reigned for fifty-five years doing evil in God's eyes. He rebuilt the altars to Baal that his father had destroyed. He practised witchcraft, soothsaying, and fortune telling. He spilled a lot of innocent blood before he died.

He was succeeded by his son Amon who also did evil in God's eyes, so his servants conspired against him and killed him.

He was followed by his son Josiah who did right in God's eyes. He and the high priest Hilkiah removed all the utensils made for Baal and burnt them. He destroyed everything that was against God. Despite all this, God was still angry with Judah, as with Israel, for the past. The Pharaoh of Egypt, Necho, killed Josiah in a battle with the Assyrians.

He was succeeded by his son Jehoahaz who ruled for only three months, before he was captured by Necho and imprisoned in Egypt where he died. He too had done evil in God's eyes.

Necho made Eliakim, the son of Josiah, the king instead and changed his name to Jehoiakim. Jehoiakim paid a heavy ransom to Pharaoh and also did evil in God's eyes. He shed a lot of innocent blood and was defeated in battle with the Syrians, Moabites, and Ammonites.

His son Jehoiachin was king for only three months, also doing evil. He was taken prisoner by Nebuchadrezzar, the king of Babylon, who stole all his treasures and took him to Babylon. Nebuchadrezzar made Mattaniah, his uncle, the new king and changed his name to Zedekiah.

Zedekiah ruled for eleven years, doing evil things just like Jehoiakim. He rebelled against Nebuchadrezzar, who then besieged Jerusalem, killed his sons, blinded him, captured him, and brought him into Babylon. Nebuchadrezzar then completely destroyed Jerusalem, including the house of the Lord, sent everybody into exile, and took away all the treasures.

The Chaldean army under Nebuzaradan, the chief officer, allowed the poorest people to remain as farmers. The chief priest and his assistants were all brought to Babylon and killed. Gedaliah was put in charge of the rest of Judah, but he was soon killed.

The next king of Babylon, Evil-merodach, took Jehoiachin out of prison and allowed him to live in Babylon until his death.

THE FIRST BOOK
OF CHRONICLES

This book starts with all the children from Adam until Saul, explaining the genealogical line and where they all settled.

After Saul committed suicide, the Philistines cut his head off and paraded his body around. They left his head at Dagon's temple. Saul died because he acted disloyally and was unfaithful to God.

David became king of Israel. He marched on to Jerusalem, which was then called Jebus. The Jebusites refused to let him in, so David captured the city, which then became the city of David. It goes on to describe all the top men in David's army and how they helped him. One of them, called Uzza, died trying to bring God's Ark to Jerusalem from Judah because he touched it. So David named the place where he died Perez-uzza. The Ark was kept in the house of Obed-edom for three months.

David twice defeated the Philistines by asking God's help, and his fame spread. He then got the Levites to bring the Ark of God into a tent and then presented burnt and peace offerings to God while the people rejoiced and sang God's praises.

David overcame the Philistines, the Moabites, the Zobahs, and the Syrians, who all became his subjects. Tou (the king of Hamath,) an enemy of Hadadezer (the king of the Syrians) brought gold, silver and bronze to David and became became David's ally. David then defeated the combined forces of the Syrians and Ammonites when they joined forces to fight him, following the death of Nahash, the Ammonite king. (David had sent emissaries to console them, but they turned around and humiliated David's men by shaving them, cutting their robes just below the belt, and sending them away.)

David sent Joab, his army chief, to do a census of Israel, making God angry so He sent an epidemic on to Israel, killing 70,000 people and almost destroying Jerusalem, but He felt sorry for the people at the last minute.

David asked for forgiveness and blamed himself, asking God to punish him alone as it was his fault. David then built an altar for God and offered burnt offerings. He then prepared everything for his son Solomon to build a Temple for God. God, however, did not allow David to build it because he had shed too much blood in his name.

David told all the elders of Israel to give assistance to Solomon then made him king of Israel as he himself was old. He took a census of all the Levites aged thirty years and above and entrusted them to work in the Temple. He handed the plans of the Temple to Solomon. Then all the clan leaders, princes, commanders, and supervisors of the king made a voluntary contribution towards the Temple.

David told everyone to praise and bless God. They gave burnt offerings, drank, ate, danced, and rejoiced as Solomon took his seat on the throne.

David died after ruling for forty years (seven years in Hebron and thirty-three years in Jerusalem).

THE SECOND BOOK
OF CHRONICLES

Solomon was asked by God what he wanted, and he asked for wisdom and knowledge, which he was granted. He started work on the Temple on Mount Moriah where the Lord had appeared to David. He also registered all the aliens in Israel. Huram, the master craftsman lent to him by Hiram, the king of Tyre, was put in charge of building the Temple.

When it was finished, Solomon assembled the elders, tribal heads, and princes of clans of the people of Israel in Jerusalem. The Levites brought up the Ark from Zion, the city of David, and put it in the Temple. The two tablets bearing the Ten Commandments were still where Moses had put them.

They then celebrated with music and sang praises to God. Solomon prayed to God to bless his people and the Temple. When he finished, fire came down from Heaven and consumed the burnt offerings and sacrifices, while the glory of the Lord filled the Temple. They then had a feast for seven days, and on the eighth day, the people held a special meeting, and everyone went home.

God appeared to Solomon and warned him to obey His Commandments and things would go well but if he didn't and served other gods, there would be problems for him and his people.

Solomon developed Israel and the surrounding areas. He also conscripted slave labour from those who were not Israelites. The queen of Sheba came to listen to Solomon's wisdom and was so impressed by what she saw that she presented him with many gifts, including gold, precious stones, and spices.

Solomon became the greatest, wisest, and richest ruler in the world. Many kings came to hear his wisdom, and each brought immense gifts. When he died, his son Rehoboam took over and was crowned at Shechem.

Jeroboam, Nebat's son, had been in Egypt where he had fled because he was afraid of Solomon. He returned to ask Rehoboam for a pardon. Rehoboam was given three days for an answer during which he consulted with the elders of Israel who advised him to look favourably to Jeroboam in the interest of peace. Jeroboam returned after three days only to be rebuffed because Rehoboam refused to listen to the elders. The Israelites split up, each to his own region. Rehoboam remained king of Judah after running away from Jerusalem. He tried to get his troops together, but God turned them all back, so he settled in Jerusalem. He fortified the cities in Judah in defence against Jeroboam.

He had eighteen wives and sixty concubines, producing twenty-eight sons and sixty daughters. Maacah was his favourite wife, so he groomed Abijah, his son by her, to follow him and made him prince.

When Rehoboam's power became established, he went against God, so Shishak, the king of Egypt, marched against him and captured his stronghold cities, advancing as far as Jerusalem. Rehoboam then repented, but Shishak still entered Jerusalem and confiscated the treasure of the Lord's Temple before leaving. God did not send total destruction on Rehoboam because he had repented, even though there were constant hostilities between him and Jeroboam. Rehoboam ruled for seventeen years and died. He was buried in the city of David, and his son Abijah became king of Judah.

Abijah ruled for three years and was constantly at war with Jeroboam. He defeated Jeroboam and captured some cities from him. He had fourteen wives, twenty-two sons, and sixteen daughters. Jeroboam was still king of Israel when Abijah died.

Asa, Abijah's son, became the new king of Judah. There was peace in his reign because he did what was good in God's eyes. He destroyed all the false altars and instructed his people to turn to God. He destroyed Zerah and his Ethiopian army with God's help and then captured all the cities around Gerah. Oded's son Azariah told Asa to stay in God's ways, otherwise calamity would fall on him. Asa gathered everybody in Judah together and made an oath to God and anyone who refused would be killed. Asa even deposed his mother, Maacah, from being queen because she worshipped an Asherah image.

Peace reigned for thirty-five years, until Baasha, the king of Israel, advanced against Judah. Asa took gold and silver and sent it to Ben-Hadad, the king of Syria, in order for him to break his treaty with Baasha. Ben-Hadad overpowered Baasha's army, and he withdrew from attacking Judah. God was angry with Asa for not relying on him. Asa fell ill and died after ruling for thirty-nine years.

His son Jehoshaphat became king. He walked in God's ways and removed all the images of other gods in Judah. God made him so rich and powerful that nobody dared to make war with him. Rather, they brought him gifts. When he felt he was rich enough, he made a marriage alliance with Ahab, the king of Israel. Together, they attacked Ramoth-gilead, the king of Syria, and Ahab was killed. God saved Jehoshaphat, who returned to his palace in Jerusalem.

Later the Moabs and Ammonites attacked Jehoshaphat's army, so he gathered the whole of Judah together to pray to God, and the Ammonites were beaten. Jehoshaphat's men collected all the booty and brought it home. They praised the Lord, rejoiced, and feasted. He reigned in Judah for twenty-five years and died after making an alliance with Ahaziah, the king of Israel who had acted wickedly and against God.

Jehoshaphat was followed by his son Jehoram, who killed all his brothers in order to strengthen his position. He married Ahab's (the wicked king of Israel) sister and did evil in God's eyes. He ruled for eight years, destroyed the Edomites who had revolted against him, and made images of other gods in high places. God did not destroy Judah because of His Covenant with David.

Elijah warned Jehoram that tragedy would fall on him for going against God. He was attacked by the Philistines, Arabians, and Ethiopians who raided Judah, plundered, and killed his wives and sons, all except Jehoahaz, the youngest. He was finally struck with an incurable intestinal disease and died.

The next king of Judah was his son Ahaziah, who also went against God and was killed by Jehu, who God had anointed to put an end to Ahab's rule in Israel. Ahaziah's mother, Athaliah, killed all the descendants of the house of Judah on hearing that her son had died, but Jehoshabeath, Ahaziah's daughter, hid Jehoash (Joash) her kid brother for six years so that he was not killed by Athaliah.

Jehoida the priest took over and made the Levites guard God's Temple. They brought out Jehoash (Joash) amidst pomp, pageantry, and rejoicing. They announced him king of Judah at the age of seven. Athaliah was caught and executed. Then Jehoida ordered all the images against God to be destroyed. They also executed Mattan, the priest of Baal, in front of the Baal temple and altars. Jehoash (Joash) collected money from everybody in Judah in order to rebuild the Lord's Temple and throughout Jehoida's lifetime, the people continued to sacrifice burnt offerings to the Lord.

When Jehoida died aged 130, Jehoash (Joash) began listening to the princes of Judah and neglected the Temple. When Jehoida's son Zechariah complained and warned them for going against God, he was stoned to death. The Syrian army came and plundered Judah, leaving Jehoash (Joash) wounded. His servants conspired against him and finally killed him in his bed.

His son Amaziah was twenty-five when he ascended to the throne and ruled for twenty-nine years doing right in God's eyes. He executed the murderers of his father. He tried to hire soldiers from Israel but was told to return them because God was against Israel. With a small army, he defeated the Edomites. The Israelite troops that he returned were incensed and raided cities in Judah, killing three thousand.

Amaziah started worshipping other gods. He challenged Joash, the king of Israel (the son of Jehoahaz and grandson of Jehu), to a battle but was defeated and captured. Joash then plundered Jerusalem. Amaziah later fled but was caught and assassinated.

His son Uzziah became king of Judah at the age of sixteen and ruled for fifty-two years. He did right in God's eyes. He defeated the Philistines, Arabians, and Meunites. The Ammonites paid tribute to him. He fortified Jerusalem and made the army strong. He then became proud and entered God's Temple to burn incense on the altars. When warned by the priests, he did not listen, and God turned him into a leper, and he spent the rest of his life in confinement.

His son Jotham became king at the age of twenty-five and reigned for sixteen years. He did right in God's eyes and defeated the Ammonites. When he died, his son Ahaz became king of Judah at the age of twenty.

Ahaz ruled for sixteen years. He did evil in God's eyes, making images and sacrifices to other gods. The king of Syria defeated him, took many prisoners, and deported them to Damascus. The king of Israel also inflicted heavy casualties on him, plundered him, and took 200,000 captives. A prophet though warned him to return the captives back to Judah or incur God's anger. He returned the captives

Ahaz stripped the Lord's Temple and made more altars to his gods. He was the most evil of the kings of Judah. When he finally died, his son Hezekiah became king at the age of twenty-five.

Hezekiah ruled for twenty-nine years, doing right in God's eyes. He repaired the Lord's Temple and sanctified it. He gave burnt offerings and slaughtered several animals in God's Name. His people then sang praises to God. He then sent word to all Israel and Judah inviting them to come to the Lord's Temple and give themselves up to God. Many came, and he prayed to God to forgive everybody. God listened to Hezekiah and healed the people.

They sacrificed animals to God, prayed, feasted, and rejoiced for there had been nothing like this since the days of

Solomon and David. After this, the people tore down and destroyed all the graven images and altars that were anti-God in Judah and Israel. Everybody contributed to God's Temple.

The king of Assyria, Sennacherib, tried to invade Judah, so Hezekiah and his priests prayed to God who annihilated all his strong fighting men, so he had to return home in disgrace and was assassinated by one of his own men.

Hezekiah became very rich and successful, and when he died, his son Manasseh took over at the age of twelve. He ruled for fifty-five years. He did evil in God's eyes, destroying all that his father had built. He worshipped Baal and practised spiritualism, fortune telling, and sorcery. He encouraged mediums and wizards, building altars and idols inside God's Temple. God spoke to him, but he would not listen, so He sent the Assyrian army on him. Manasseh was captured and taken to Babylon.

Manasseh then humbled himself and prayed, acknowledging that the Lord is indeed God, and he was restored to Jerusalem. He removed the foreign gods and images from the Temple and ordered his people to serve only God. When he died, his son Amon became king at the age of twenty-two.

Amon ruled for two years, doing evil in God's eyes. He did not humble himself to God as his father had done and was assassinated. His son Josiah became king at the age of eight.

Josiah ruled for thirty-one years. He did what was right in God's eyes. He destroyed all the altars and graven images that were against God. He collected money from his people and rebuilt the Lord's Temple. As they were cleaning out the Temple, they found the Lord's Book of Law that was given through Moses, which stated that Judah and Israel would be destroyed because they had sinned and had not listened to God. Hilkiah, the priest, went to Huldah, the prophetess, who said that because Josiah had humbled himself to God, he would be saved and die in peace.

Josiah affirmed his faith in God, destroyed all the detestable things in his lands, and ordered everyone to follow the Lord. He never deviated in his ways. He put the Holy Ark back in the Temple. He observed the Passover, sacrificing many things for God. His people then rejoiced and held a feast for seven days.

When Neco, the king of Egypt, came for a battle, Josiah went to fight him against God's wishes and was mortally wounded. He was brought back to Jerusalem, where he died.

His son Jehoahaz was twenty-three when he became king and ruled for only three months when he was deposed by Neco and taken to Egypt. Neco made his brother Eliakim the new king of Judah, changing his name to Jehoiakim.

Jehoiakim was twenty-five when he became king, and he ruled for eleven years. He did what was wrong in God's eyes and was attacked by Nebuchadrezzar, the king of Babylon. He was defeated and taken to Babylon in chains. Nebuchadrezzar also looted the Lord's Temple.

Jehoiachin (the son of Jehoiakim) became king of Judah at eighteen and ruled for only three months and ten days, doing wrong in God's eyes. He was deposed by Nebuchadrezzar and taken to Babylon with the rest of the precious things from the Lord's Temple.

Jehoiachin's uncle Zedekiah became king of Judah at the age of twenty-one and ruled for eleven years. He also did evil in God's eyes and did not heed the warnings of Jeremiah the prophet. He rebelled against Nebuchadrezzar, desecrated the Lord's Temple, continued his evil practices with other gods, and made fun of all the priests and God's messengers till God's patience ran out.

Nebuchadrezzar, the king of the Chaldeans, attacked Judah, killed most of the people, destroyed Jerusalem, looted the Lord's Temple, and took all the survivors captive to Babylon, where they became slaves to him until the kingdom of Persia came to power, seventy years later.

In order to fulfil what Jeremiah the prophet had said, Cyrus, the king of Persia, was commissioned by God to build a new Temple for the Lord in Jerusalem.

THE BOOK OF EZRA

Cyrus, the king of Persia, in his first year told everybody who belonged to Judah that they could return in order to rebuild God's Temple. He also returned all the gold and silver stolen by Nebuchadrezzar to Jerusalem. All the people returned, bringing gifts, animals, and precious things in order to rebuild the city. They built an altar to God, presented burnt offerings, and sang praises before building the Temple.

In the days of Artaxerxes, the new king of Persia, the enemies got him to stop them building the Temple because it would make Jerusalem too powerful. They presented a letter to the Jews, and the work was stopped. They also did the same when Ahasuerus was king of Persia.

When Darius became king of Persia, Haggai the prophet and Zechariah began preaching to the Jews in Jerusalem in God's Name, and, helped by Zerubbabel and Jeshua, they began to build the Lord's Temple, which was completed in the sixth year of Darius' reign. Darius had given his wholehearted support because of what Cyrus had decreed. There was feasting and rejoicing for seven days after the Temple was completed.

Ezra, a descendant of Aaron, left Babylon with many followers to Jerusalem. He was a man of God, well versed in the Law of Moses. He was given a letter from King Artaxerxes of Persia to facilitate his journey and permission to collect any riches and animals from Babylon to Jerusalem.

Ezra made his followers fast and pray along the way at the Ahava River because he was ashamed to ask the king for horses and troops, since he had told him that the hand of God would protect them.

On arrival, the people started intermarrying and conducting themselves in evil practices, like their forefathers. Ezra was upset and went into the house of God. He fasted, tore his clothes, pulled out his hair, lay on the ground, cried, and

prayed to God to stop them behaving in that way. The people were so moved that they decided to change and make a
covenant with God to change. Ezra finally got up and made
everybody swear to change (which they did), before he left
the house of God.

He gave all the men in Judah three days to assemble in
front of him and told them to have nothing more to do with
all the men who had married foreign women so that God's
anger would be turned away from them.

THE BOOK OF NEHEMIAH

Nehemiah was in captivity in Persia when he was saddened by the plight of Jerusalem. He got permission from King Artaxerxes to go back to Jerusalem and rebuild it. The king gave him letters addressed to his governors to facilitate his journey. He prayed to God before going, and when he arrived, he got the people together to rebuild the wall. Enemies of the Jews tried to stop them with threats, but God scattered their evil plans. They continued building it, while arming themselves.

The people then complained about their hunger, lack of property, and the taxes they had been paying to the nobles and rulers. Nehemiah confronted them, and they gave back the land and possessions to their rightful owners.

Nehemiah was appointed governor of Judah, and he pressed on and finished the building of the wall. The enemies of Judah led by Sanballat and Tobiah did their best to frighten Nehemiah and to lure him into a trap and kill him, but God was with him, and they failed in all their plans, including trying to get influential men in Judah itself to go against him.

Nehemiah then registered his people. Ezra gathered them in one place for seven days while he explained God's Laws from the book of Moses to them. They all praised God and rejoiced. Ezra made them all get tents to sleep in during the festival.

Later on in the month, the people were again brought together and prayed to God, confessing their sins, thanking God for saving them, and promising to follow Him. The priests set their seal on this promise. Since the leaders of the people all lived in Jerusalem, lots were cast to bring one out of ten inhabitants from all the other towns to come and live there too. The book of Moses was read to all the newcomers.

Nehemiah, on his return from visiting King Artaxerxes in Babylon, came to God's Temple and found it unattended and some people treading wine presses on the Sabbath day. He reproved the leaders for allowing this to happen because God would be angry with the whole town.

He also forced the Jews who had married foreigners to take an oath in the Name of God and made them promise not to intermarry again.

He established the duties of the priests and of the Levites who were supposed to look after the Temple. Nehemiah, at the end of this book, asks God to remember him kindly for all that he did for Judah.

THE BOOK OF ESTHER

After Ahasuerus' Queen Vashti disobeyed him, he removed her as queen and invited a group of virgins to come to him so that he could pick the best and most beautiful in order to make her the new queen. Prompted by her stepfather Mordecai, a Jew, Esther took the king's fancy, and he made her queen, throwing a big banquet in her honour.

Mordecai helped foil an attempted coup by two of the king's eunuchs, Bigthan and Teresh, by telling Esther, who warned the king. The king then promoted Haman as the head of his princes after having the two eunuchs hanged for their treason.

Haman, however, used the king's name to send an edict all over his domain for all the deputies to kill any Jew that they saw and to take his property. When Mordecai heard about it, he dressed in sackcloth and lamented. Word got to Queen Esther, and she pleaded with the king to spare Mordecai because it was he who had foiled the plot against the king.

Esther planned a big banquet and told the king about Haman's treachery against the Jews. Haman was hanged on the very gallows he had built to hang Mordecai on.

Mordecai became the king's new right hand man. He and Esther sent an edict in the king's name to reverse Haman's order for the Jews to be killed. Meanwhile, the Jews themselves had united and turned on their enemies, killing all of them.

Peace reigned in Ahasuerus' one hundred twenty-seven provinces, thanks to Esther and Mordecai.

THE BOOK OF JOB

A rich, God-loving and God-fearing man in the land of Uz, who had everything, was tested by God through Satan. He used to offer burnt offerings and pray to God in order for Him to forgive the sins of his ten children. When all his animals, property, and children were destroyed by attacks from the Chaldeans and the elements, Job tore his clothes, shaved his head, and still worshipped God. So Satan struck him with a horrible disease, but he still refused to go against God.

Three of his friends, Eliphaz, Bildad, and Zopher, sat on the ground with him for seven days without speaking to him as he was suffering. Then Job finally cursed the day he was born, saying that it would have been better if he had died at birth. His friends then admonished him for losing faith in God. Eliphaz explained that God is everything. He punishes, He saves, He wounds, He heals, He redeems. In short, if one were to forsake God, where would one go to?

Job answered that the way he was, it would have been better if he were dead. Why should God treat him in this way? He was completely helpless, with no chance of recovery. If there was a better way for him to appeal to God to end his torment, they should tell him. If he has done any harm to God, then He should end his suffering, but they should not waste their time giving him advice because he would soon be dead.

Bildad then said that he should stop talking like that; God does not twist justice. If one is good, one will be rewarded. One cannot be punished for somebody else's sins. The godless man will perish, and everything he does will come to nothing. One should be patient, and God will reward him and his enemies will be ashamed.

Job replied that a mortal cannot be right in front of God. No one can dispute God's decisions. God is the creator of everything, so He knows why He does anything. Why should he bother wondering whether he is guilty or not or why God has treated him like that? God made him, and when He wants to, He will destroy him. Why did God even bother to create him and watch him sin, only to destroy him? It would have been better if he had not been born. His days were few and numbered. They should leave him alone and let him die in peace.

Then Zophar said that one cannot fight God or know the way He does things so instead of complaining, one should give himself to God and He will banish sin from one's life, and one will have no trouble or fear. God always holds less against us than our iniquities deserve.

Job then replied that he was human like them and knew all that they were saying. Why should they side with God? Everyone knows that God controls everything. Even the people who sin are given good things and prosperity by God. If anything, they should stop being partial to God and let him argue his own case with God Himself. He had prepared his case, and he was sure that he would be vindicated. What was certain was that he was a dried up lake who would one day die and not get up again. Even a tree has hope because if it is cut down, it will sprout up again.

Eliphaz replied that Job was a nobody to talk against God. What does a mere mortal know about the way God works? There are even older and wiser men than he, and they don't know everything. As the heavens are not pure in God's eyes, how could a mere human being be pure? Wicked men are tormented all their lives, and those who go against God will always suffer.

Then Job answered that he'd heard such things before and that they were all miserable comforters. Whether he speaks or not, his suffering will be the same. He could talk like them if he were in their shoes. They were not the ones suffering. He was living a life of ease until God made him a laughing stock, sent him into the hands of the godless and broke him down, turning him into this pitiful sight. His life was ruined, and he was just waiting for his grave.

Bildad then said that those who don't acknowledge God will always fall into traps and pitfalls and whatever they gain will quickly disappear and nothing of theirs will ever last long. Job was tearing himself into a rage, and things would never change just for his sake.

Job asked them how long would they keep on pestering him without feeling any shame? If he had done wrong then his error will remain with him. God has misjudged him because he cries for help, but no one answers him. God robbed him of his honour, broke him down, uprooted him like a tree, and removed his brothers and acquaintances from him. His friends, relatives, servants, and even wife had forgotten him, so why should they persecute him too? Aren't they satisfied with what they are seeing? They should be careful because their attitude could bring suffering upon themselves so that they would know there was a judgement.

Zophar replied that he had heard his presumptuous warning to stop advising him, but a spirit prompted him to continue. Since man has been on earth, the triumph of the wicked was always brief and the joys of the godless only momentary. His pride may be lofty, but when he dies, who will remember him? He will quickly disappear from people's memory. His children will give away his wealth. He will vomit all the riches that he has swallowed. Everything he has worked for must be given up, and what he acquires through trading will not bring him any joy. With all his wealth, he will still be miserable. If God lets His anger loose on him, everything that he has accumulated will be lost, and the earth will rise up against him.

Job asked but why do the wicked always live long and prosper without any problems? God's rod never strikes them. They always die in peace. What does one gain by serving God or appealing to Him? Men are not architects of their own fortune. If God stores up one's iniquities for his children, then the wicked will not be worried and will not care when they are dead. Both rich and poor must die and be bur-

ied in the same ground for the worms, so how can they expect to comfort him when they are all talking rubbish?

Eliphaz answered that it was not any advantage to God
whether one is perfect or not. One's sin is endless. That is not
why he (Job) is really suffering. God is in Heaven so high up
that he cannot see Him yet he wants to challenge Him and
ask why he does certain things. He should get closer to Him
and enjoy His love. He should throw away all his gold and
precious things and come to Him because God exalts the
humble man and saves him.

Job then answered that he wished he could find God and
present his case, in order to find out what He would say so
that he could understand Him better. He looked everywhere
and cannot see God, yet he has been true to Him and kept
His ways. God always does what He wants to do and He will
carry out what He has planned for him. There are men who
kill, steal, commit adultery, and do all kinds of bad things,
but God still allows them and even gives them confidence
while they are alive and then they are gone . . . withered
away like everyone else!

Bildad reiterated that no one can be mightier than God.
We are but mere mortals.

Job then said that for someone who is a mere mortal, he
really knew how to advise the weak and feeble. Who gave
him such wisdom and by whose spirit was he inspired? As
long as God lives, he (Job) will never lie. What hope is there
for the godless when God Himself cuts him off? Will they
call to God for help? What has happened is God's way of
punishing the wicked. There is no need to indulge in any
more futility. Everything was done with God's Hand. One
always got what one deserved.

The earth was full of riches, which man is always looking for. He drills holes in the earth, overturns mountains,
dams up streams, and unearths precious stones, but he cannot find true wisdom nor does he know its value. Gold cannot purchase it or equal it. Only God knows the way to do

it. Reverence to God is wisdom, and departure from evil is understanding.

Before, he was rich, respected, in the prime of his life, protected by God and he helped children, the poor, the sick and the aged. People came to him for advice. Now they derided him, spit on him, and showed him no respect but scorn. They teased him, and no one stopped them. He had pains in his body, and his clothes were in rags. He cried to God for help but received no answer. He only knew that he would soon die, and he would go to where the dead people go. He did what he could. If he had done any wrong then he should be punished by the Almighty.

Elihu, one of his friends, became angry and decided to express his own views. He was angry with Job for putting his own feelings before God's, and with Eliphaz, Bildad, and Zophar for not having a good answer for Job yet they were saying that he was wrong. Elihu had not said anything before because he felt, being younger than they, he should let them speak first.

He said that God speaks in different ways and protects us in more ways than we will ever know. Nobody knows what happens when we sleep. God gives us warnings in our sleep so that we don't die. Job is not being fair to God when he claims he has not done anything wrong and is being punished by God. He, Elihu, will now teach him wisdom.

He continued by saying that God does not do wrong or bad. He made the world, and if He were to withdraw His Spirit, we would all die. He doesn't favour the rich any more than the poor. All men must one day die and face God's Judgement. Only He knows when to take and to give. Evildoers cannot hide because God sees everything. He remains quiet. No one can see Him or touch Him, but He watches over all nations and individuals. Nothing is too petty for Him. Job does not speak intelligently and adds rebellion to his sins.

No one is more righteous than God. Whether you sin, or do good, the sky remains the same yet nothing happens without God. We shouldn't think that because we cannot see God, He does not look after us. Job just opens his mouth and utters useless statements. God will never prolong the life of the wicked, but He will always give a wronged person his right. He lets people know where they have gone wrong and gives them chances to correct their faults. If they pay no attention then they will perish, but if they listen to God then they will live a long and happy life.

Suffering is a test to see if one will turn to evil. Love, worship and glorify God because He is great and has been around longer than anyone can imagine. Who understands the wind, the clouds, thunder and lightning? He does great things that we will never be able to understand. God is powerful and fair so we should revere Him because He will not respect anyone who is conceited.

God then asked Job from a whirlwind, *"Where were you when I founded the earth? Who determined its measurements? Who made the sea? Do you know where the light or darkness comes from? Have you ever seen death? What is snow, rain, or ice? Are you the one who determines the seasons or the universe? What about the habits of all the animals and birds? Who makes sure their young are looked after when the parents have not been given enough intelligence to feed or protect them? Can you contend with the Almighty?"*

Job then said that he is too small to say anything, so he would not complain anymore.

God continued, *"Will you discredit My Justice? Get up and cover yourself with honour and majesty. Crush the wicked, walk with pride and I will praise you because you can look after yourself. You should be as strong, as fearless, and as confident as a hippopotamus, the foremost in My ways. A crocodile is so tough that man cannot do anything with it. No weapon can harm it. No human can ever come close to him. I made the crocodile so who can stand in front of Me? I have not borrowed anything from anyone and so I don't owe anyone anything. Everything is Mine because I made it."*

Job then confessed to God that he was wrong and re-pented. God then told Eliphaz, Bildad, and Zophar to offer burnt offerings for themselves and to ask Job to pray for them because they did not tell the truth about Him. They did as He asked, and God forgave them.

God then gave back Job's possessions and doubled his fortune and property. All his brothers, sisters, and friends came back to him to eat in his house. God blessed his latter days even more than the earlier ones, and Job had seven sons and three daughters. He lived a full life and died an old man at the age of 140.

THE BOOK OF PSALMS

It is almost impossible to try to explain what each Psalm is all about. There are 150 of them, and I have managed to put them into groups. The best way to understand the Psalms is to read each one separately and hopefully they will have some meaning for you. Each one will have a different significance to every individual, depending on one's circumstances in life. They are, however, a great source of comfort and inspiration. The Psalms express the whole range of human feeling and experience, from dark depression to exuberant joy. They all relate to particular circumstances that have been the same over the ages. The human being is still stirred by the same emotions as in the past. We still have the same fundamental problems of life, and we still cry out for help to the same God as in the past. The sheer expression of faith and love of God in the Psalms is a real tonic in this ever-increasingly violent and loveless world.

The Psalms is a collection of five books: 1–41, 42–72, 73–89, 90–106, and 107–150. Each book ends with a little praise to God. Within the five books, the Psalms are often grouped into common themes, a common purpose, or a common author.

Seventy-three psalms are attributed to King David, some collected by him and the rest dedicated to him as the king. Many of them are to do with musical instruments and musical settings, which are difficult to understand at the best of times.

There are psalms that plead with God, and psalms that praise Him and celebrate the greatness of His Law. Some appeal for the forgiveness or the destruction of enemies, while others are prayers for the king or the nation. All, however, are part of the religious life of Israel.

Examples of the psalms that praise God's character and deeds are: Psalms, 8, 19, and 29.

Examples of psalms about community laments arising out of national disasters are: Psalms 44 and 74.

Examples of psalms dedicated to some occasion in the life of the reigning king are: Psalms 2, 18, 20, and 45.

Examples of psalms to do with individual laments are: 3, 7, 13, 25, and 51.

Examples of psalms that are individual thanksgivings are: 30, 32, and 34.

Psalm 23 is perhaps the most famous, probably because it has been turned into a popular hymn. Psalm 119 is the longest with 176 verses, and Psalms 131 and 133, with three verses each, are the shortest.

THE BOOK OF PROVERBS

These are the proverbs written by Solomon showing one how to gain wisdom and instruction in prudence and uprightness, know right from wrong, and truly understand justice. There are many of these proverbs, and many are repeated throughout the book. What I have done is pick quite a few of them, based on different aspects of life in order to have a general view of what they are all about. You will have to consult a Bible in order to be able to read all of them.

A wise man will listen and increase his knowledge. Reverence of the Lord is the beginning of knowledge. Listen to your parents and don't follow sinners or wicked people. Waywardness of the simple brings death, and self-assurance of fools brings their destruction. Follow God's Commandments and accept His Word, and He will protect, advise, and instruct you. Trust in God with all your heart, don't rely on your own understanding, and He will show you the right way to go. God loves those He corrects so don't despise His discipline. Wisdom is more valuable than jewellery, gold, or silver. God founded the earth by wisdom and established the heavens by understanding. Honour God with the first products of your income. Keep sound wisdom and discretion, and you will walk confidently without fear and never stumble. Love your neighbour and don't envy a violent man. God's curse is on the wicked, but He blesses the righteous. The wise will inherit honour.

Don't follow evil, but watch over your heart, which is the source of your life. Don't follow loose women or you will lose your wealth to those who don't work for it. Drink only from your own tank. Be satisfied with your own wife and don't go in for somebody else's wife, or you will lose your honour and your life. If you have said something bad to your neighbour, humble yourself and go to his house and apologise. A wicked and worthless man is one who is always devising evil, sowing discord, and lying. He will soon be broken, and there will be no cure.

God hates proud eyes, a lying tongue, hands shedding innocent blood, hearts devising wicked schemes, feet quick to run to evil, a false witness, and he who sows discord. Honour your mother and father and keep away from the beauty of a loose woman, or you will be burnt. She draws an unsuspecting man to the slaughter with her sophistries. God also hates pride, arrogance, and all evil ways.

Solomon once said that God gave him wisdom, riches, and honour, so we should listen to him and we will be happy. Those who find Him find life and win approval from Him. Quit the company of the simple and walk in the way of the understanding. If you correct a scorner, he will heap abuse on to you. Likewise, if you reprove a wicked man, he will hate you. Reprove a wise man, and he will love you.

Reverence of God is the beginning of wisdom, and knowledge of God is understanding. If you are wise, you benefit yourself, and if you scorn people, you will get it back on yourself alone.

A foolish woman is noisy, simple, and knows nothing. Wickedness brings no profit, but righteousness saves one from death. God does not let the soul of the righteous go hungry, but he frustrates the desire of the wicked. The mouth of the wicked conceals violence. He who walks in integrity walks securely, but he who takes a crooked course will be found out. The prating fool will always fall down.

Hatred stirs up contentions, but love covers all transgressions. Wise men always store up knowledge. He who listens to instruction will stay on the path of life, but he who refuses to listen to reproof will go astray. The foolish perish from a lack of understanding. It is God's blessing that brings riches. Hard work will add nothing to it.

What the wicked fears will come to him, but the desire of the righteous will be granted. The expectations of the wicked will come to nothing. Reverence of God adds many days to one's life, but the years of the wicked will be shortened. The wicked person falls by his own wickedness. The righteousness of the upright delivers them, but the treacherous are trapped by their own greediness. The righteous person will be delivered from trouble, and the wicked person will take his place.

A kindly man does himself good, but a troublemaker hurts himself. He who pursues evil brings about his own death. The evil man will not go unpunished, but the offspring of the righteous will escape. The charitable soul will be enriched, and he who waters will himself be watered. He who trusts in his riches will fall. The righteous will be repaid on earth; how much more the wicked and the sinner! The wicked will be overthrown and die, but the house of the righteous will stand. A man is commended for his common sense, but a man with twisted thoughts will be hated.

A wise man always listens to advice. A fool's displeasure is immediately known, but a wise man ignores an insult. Truthful lips last forever, but a lying tongue lasts only for the wink of an eye. The righteous will come to no harm, but the wicked will be filled with trouble. A man of insight conceals his knowledge, but the heart of fools proclaims foolishness. The hand of the diligent will rule, but the slack hand will be forced to serve. A wise son accepts his father's correction, but a scorner does not listen to rebuke.

He who guards his mouth controls himself, but he who opens wide his lips comes to ruin. Wisdom is with those who take advice. Wealth acquired rashly dwindles away, but he who works hard will increase his wealth. He who despises the Word will be in debt to it, and he who respects the Commandment will be rewarded. A person of insight acts with forethought, but a fool displays his folly.

Poverty and shame will come to those who refuse instruction, but the one who listens to reproof will be honoured. Calamity pursues sinners, but the righteous are rewarded with prosperity. A good man leaves an inheritance to his children's children. He who spares his rod hates his son, but he who loves him is careful to correct him with punishment.

The righteous person eats to satisfy his need, but the wicked's stomach never has enough. A wise woman builds her own house, but a foolish one tears it down with her own hands.

Leave the presence of a man who is a fool, for you will not learn any words of knowledge there. The wisdom of a man of insight is in his anticipating his way. The bond between foolish men is guilt, but between the upright it is goodwill. The heart knows its own bitterness, and no stranger can intermingle with its joy. The house of the wicked shall be overthrown, but the tent of the upright shall prosper. There is a way that seems right to a person, but its end is the way of death.

Even in laughter, the heart may be sad and joy may eventuate in grief. The simple man believes everything he hears, but the man of insight makes sure where he is going. A wise man is cautious and avoids misfortune, but a fool parades himself and feels confident. He who is quick tempered acts foolishly, and a man who plans wickedness is hated. He who hates his neighbour commits a sin, but he who is gracious to the humble will be happy.

There is profit in hard work, but mere talk only leads to want. The crown of the wise is their wealth of wisdom, but the folly of fools is still folly. In reverence for the Lord, one will have strong confidence and there will be refuge for his children.

Reverence for the Lord is the fountain of life that will deliver him from the snares of death. He who is slow to anger is of great understanding, but whoever has a hasty spirit will be a fool. A relaxed mind is great for physical health, but passion is rottenness to the bones.

He who oppresses the poor insults his Maker, and he who is kind to the needy honours Him. The wicked will be overthrown by their own mischief-making, but the righteous will have confidence even while dying. Wisdom quietly rests in the heart of a man of understanding, but it has to establish itself in the inner self of fools. The king's favour is towards the servant who deals wisely, but his anger is evidenced towards he who acts shamefully.

A pleasant answer turns away anger, but a harsh word rather stirs up trouble. The eyes of the Lord are everywhere, observing the evil and the good. A soothing tongue is the tree of life, while perversity in it breaks down the spirit.

In the house of the righteous is great treasure, but the income of the wicked is full of trouble. The sacrifice of the wicked is an abomination to the Lord, but the prayer of the upright is His delight. God loves those who are righteous. There is severe discipline for those who forsake the way, and those who hate reproof will die. A scorner does not like to be rebuked, so he will not go to the wise.

All the days of the poor are unfortunate, but the glad hearted has a continual feast. Better a little with reverence for the Lord, than great treasure and lamentation without it. Better a vegetable meal where love is, than a fattened ox and hatred with it. A hot-tempered man causes trouble, but one who is slow to anger quiets contention. A wise son makes his father glad, but a foolish man despises his mother. Folly is joy to one who lacks sense, but a discerning man takes a straight course. Plans go wrong with lack of advice but are accomplished with many counsellors.

The Lord tears down the house of the proud man, but He protects the boundaries of the widow. Wicked thoughts are an abomination to the Lord, but kindly words are pure. He who plunders for profit troubles his own house, but the one who hates bribes will live. The mind of the righteous man thinks before answering, but the mouth of the wicked pours out evil things.

God hears the prayer of the righteous but is far from the wicked. He who ignores correction despises himself, and he who listens to reproof acquires intelligence. Reverence of the Lord is the instruction of wisdom, but before honour, there must be humility.

Orderly thinking belongs to man, but the answer of the tongue is from the Lord. All the ways of a man are clean in

His eyes, but the Lord weighs the spirits. Roll your work on to the Lord and your plans will be achieved. The Lord has made everything for His purpose, and has saved the wicked for the day of calamity. A proud heart is an abomination to the Lord and be assured that he who has one will not go unpunished.

Iniquity is atoned for by loyal love and faithfulness, but turning from evil comes through reverence for the Lord. When the ways of a man please the Lord, He makes even his enemies to be at peace with him. A man's mind plans his road, but the Lord directs his steps. The balance and scales of justice belong to the Lord. It is much better to have wisdom than gold, and it is also better to choose understanding than to choose silver.

He who trusts in the Lord will be happy. He who is slow to anger is better than the mighty hero, and he who rules his spirit is better than he who captures a city.

A slave who acts wisely will rule over the son who acts shamefully, and he will share the inheritance with the sons. He who makes fun of the poor, insults his Maker, and he who rejoices at another's calamity will not go unpunished. He who forgets an offence seeks love, but he who again brings up a matter alienates a close friend. A bribe is a precious stone in the eyes of the one receiving it; whatever he turns to, he causes to succeed.

A rebuke goes deeper into a man of understanding than a hundred blows into a fool. A wicked man seeks only rebellion, but a stern messenger will be sent against him. Calamity will not leave the house of he who returns evil for good. The beginning of strife is like letting out water, so quit before the quarrel breaks out. A friend is perpetually friendly, and a brother is born for adversity. A man without good judgement is he who makes an agreement to become a surety in the presence of his neighbour.

He who loves transgression loves trouble, and he who opens his mouth wide seeks destruction. A man of crooked mind does not find prosperity, and he who has a perverted tongue will tumble into trouble. A cheerful heart makes a good cure. A wicked man accepts a personal bribe to pervert the ways of justice.

He who restrains his words has knowledge, and he who is calm of spirit is a man of understanding. Even a fool when he is silent is thought to be wise, and he who keeps his lips closed is considered intelligent.

He who wilfully separates himself seeks his own desire and breaks out against all sound wisdom. A fool does not delight in understanding but only in revealing his own opinion. The wicked brings contempt with him, and his disdain brings reproach. It is not good to show partiality to the wicked and deprive a righteous man of justice. The lips of a fool lead to strife, and his mouth calls for a beating. A fool's mouth is his ruin, and his lips are a snare to his soul.

The Name of the Lord is a strong tower into which the righteous run where they cannot be touched. The rich man's wealth is his strong city and his high wall . . . so he thinks!

Before destruction, a man's heart is haughty, but before honour goes humility. A man's spirit will endure sickness, but who can carry a broken spirit? A discerning man gets knowledge, and the ear of the wise seeks information.

He who states his case first seems right until another comes to examine him. A brother offended is harder to be won than a strong city. Death and life are in the power of the tongue, and those who love it will eat its product.

He who has found a wife has gained a goodly portion and obtains favour from the Lord. The poor use entreaties, but the rich answer roughly. He who hurries his feet misses his mark. The foolishness of man ruins his affairs, but his heart is resentful towards the Lord. Wealth adds many friends; but as for the poor, his only friend leaves him.

A false witness will not go unpunished, and he who breathes out lies will not escape. Many will entreat the favour of a generous man, and everyone is the friend of the man who gives gifts. All the brothers of the poor despise him, and his friends go far from him; he pursues them with words, but they are gone. He who gains wisdom loves his own life, and he who maintains insight finds success.

It is prudent for a man to restrain his anger, and it is his glory to overlook an offence. A foolish son is a calamity to his father, and the quarrelling of a wife is like a constant dripping of water. House and wealth are inherited from fathers, but a prudent wife is from the Lord.

Laziness makes one sleep heavily. An idle person will suffer hunger. He who keeps the Commandments keeps his own soul, but he who despises His Way shall die. He who is gracious to the poor is lending to the Lord, who will repay him for his benevolent action. Discipline your son, for there is hope and do not set your heart on his destruction.

A man who gets angry too easily must bear the penalty. Hear advice and accept instruction so that you may be wise for the rest of your days. Many schemes are in a man's mind, but the counsel of the Lord will stand. What is desired in a man is steadfast love, for a poor man is better than a liar.

Reverence for the Lord leads to life, and he who remains satisfied with that will never come to any harm. A son who slanders his father and drives out his mother acts shamefully and disgracefully.

Judgement is ready for scorners and flogging for the back of fools. Wine is a scorner, strong drink a brawler, and whoever gets drunk is not wise.

The fury of a king is like the roaring of a lion; he who makes him angry endangers his own life. It is an honour for a man to keep away from trouble, but foolish men are always quarrelling. He who walks righteously in his integrity . . . how happy are his children after him! Who in this world can say, *"I have made my heart clean, and I am pure from sin?"* Even a child reveals himself by his acts, if what he does is pure and right. The Lord made both the hearing ear and the seeing eye.

Do not be over fond of sleep lest you come to poverty. Keep your eyes open, and you will have plenty of food. Food gained by deceit is sweet to a man, but afterwards his mouth will be filled with gravel. He who goes around telling tales reveals secrets; therefore do not associate with he who opens his lips wide. He who curses his father or his mother will have his lamp put out in utter darkness.

An estate may be obtained hastily in the beginning, but its end will not be blessed. Do not say, "*I will repay evil.*" Wait for the Lord and He will save you. A man's steps are ordered by the Lord, so how then can he understand His way? The glory of young men is their strength, and the attractiveness of old men is their grey head. Blows that wound, cleanse away evil and are strokes that reach the innermost parts.

In his own eyes, every way of a man is right, but the Lord weighs hearts. To practise righteousness and justice is more acceptable to the Lord than sacrifice. Haughty eyes, a lustful heart, and the work of the wicked are all sins. The plans of the diligent lead only to abundance, but everyone who is hasty will end up in need. The getting of riches by a lying tongue is a fleeting vapour and a pursuit of death. It is better to live in the corner of a house top than to share a house with a contentious woman.

The violence of the wicked will trap them, because they refuse to act with fairness. The righteous man deals considerately with the wicked man who will be ruined. He who closes his ears to the cry of the poor will himself also cry and not be heard. A gift in secret quiets anger, and a present in the bosom calms fury. A man who strays from the way of prudence will find rest in the assembly of the dead. He who loves pleasure will be a poor man. He who loves wine will not be rich. It is better to live in the desert land than with a contentious and fretful woman.

He who follows after righteousness and loving kindness finds life, righteousness, and honour. He who guards his mouth and his tongue keeps his soul from troubles. The desire of the sluggard will kill him because his hands refuse to work. The sluggard feels greedy all day long, but the righteous gives and does not hold back.

The sacrifice of the wicked is an abomination; how much more when he brings it with evil intent. A false witness will perish, but a man who listens faithfully will be at liberty to speak. A wicked man has an impudent face, but the upright always ponders his ways.

There is no wisdom, counsel, or understanding against the Lord. A good name is to be chosen rather than great riches, and loving favour is better than silver or gold. The rich and the poor meet together because the Lord is the Maker of them all. A prudent man sees danger and hides himself, but the simple continue on and suffer for it.

The results of humility and reverence for the Lord are riches, honour, and life. Thorns and snares are in the way of the perverse, and he who guards his soul will go far from them. Educate a child according to his life's requirements, because even when he is old, he will not veer from it. The rich rule over the poor while the borrower is a slave to the lender.

He who sows injustice will reap nothing. He who is generous and gives to the poor will be blessed. He who loves purity of heart and whose speech is pleasant will have the king as his friend. The eyes of the Lord protect knowledge, and He turns aside the words of the treacherous. The mouth of strange women is a deep pit, and he who is cursed of the Lord will fall into it.

Foolishness is bound up in the heart of a child, but the rod of discipline will drive it far from him. He who oppresses the poor to make gain for himself, or he who gives to the rich will always suffer want. Incline your ear and listen to the words of the wise.

Do not rob the poor because he is poor, nor oppress the afflicted in the gate because the Lord will plead their cause and He will take the lives of those killing them.

Do not associate with one given to anger. Do not give pledges that are securities for debts; if you do not have the means to pay, why should your bed be taken from under you? Do not desire the delicacies of the ruler, for they are deceptive food. Do not toil to get wealth; surrender that personal ambition. Riches surely take wings like an eagle that flies heavenward.

Don't eat the bread of the one whose eye is selfish, neither desire his delicacies. Do not speak to the ears of a fool, for he will despise the wisdom of your words. Apply your heart to instruction and your ears to the words of knowledge. Don't withhold correction from a child; if you beat him with a rod, he will not die, but you will deliver his soul from the devil. If your heart is wise and your lips speak what is right, then God's heart will rejoice.

Do not envy sinners but continue in the reverence of the Lord all day, and there will be a future for you, and your hope will not be cut off. Don't mix with the wine bibbers and gluttonous eaters of flesh, for the drunkard and the glutton will be poverty stricken, and drowsiness will clothe a man with rags. Heed your father, and don't despise your mother when she is old. Buy the truth and do not sell it, the same with wisdom, instruction, and understanding.

If you spend too long on wine, your eyes will see strange things and your mind will utter upside down things. Don't be envious of evil men nor desire to be with them for their minds devise violence and their lips speak mischief. A house is built by wisdom, is established by understanding, and the rooms are filled with all precious and pleasant riches, by knowledge. A wise man is strong, and a man of knowledge adds to his strength. Wisdom is too high for the foolish to understand.

If you faint in the day of adversity, it means that your strength is small. Deliver those who are being taken to their death; and from those staggering towards slaughter, will you withhold yourself? God sees everything and will repay each man for his deeds.

Eat honey for it is good and sweet. Wisdom is the same for the soul; if you have found it, then there will be a future, and your hope will not be cut off. Don't lie in wait or do violence to the house of the righteous, for he may fall seven times and yet arise, but the wicked will stumble headlong into adversity.

When your enemy falls, do not rejoice, and when he stumbles, don't be glad lest the Lord see it, and it appear wrong in His eyes, and He turn away His anger from him on to you. There is no future for the evil man. The lamp of the wicked will always burn out. Do not mingle with those given to change for their calamity will suddenly arise, and who knows the ruin that will come to both of you?

Those who rebuke the wicked will find delight, and a good blessing will come on to them. To give the right answer is like a kiss on the lips. Don't be a witness against your neighbour without just cause. Don't say, "*As he did to me, so I will do to him.*" Argue your cause with your neighbour, but do not reveal the secret of another, lest the one hearing you put you to shame and your bad reputation will be there forever.

A faithful messenger refreshes the soul of his master. When one is slow to anger, a ruler is persuaded, but soft speech will break a bone. Eat only what you need, lest being filled with it, you vomit it up. Let your foot be rarely in your neighbour's house lest he become weary of you and hate you. Don't trust a faithless man in times of adversity. If your enemy is hungry, give him bread to eat; if he is thirsty give him water to drink; for live coals will heap upon his head and the Lord will reward you. An angry face brings out a concealed tongue.

Good news from a far country is like cold water to a weary soul. A righteous man who gives way to the wicked is like a trampled fountain or a polluted spring. It is not good for men to seek their own glory. A man whose spirit is without restraint is like a city whose wall is broken down. A place of honour is not fitting for a fool. Don't answer a fool according to his folly, lest you too be like him. If you answer a fool according to his folly, he will be wise in his own eyes. He who sends a message by the hand of a fool cuts off his own feet and drinks poison. A fool will always repeat his folly. There is more hope for a fool than for a man who is wise in his own eyes.

Don't involve yourself in a quarrel that is not your own. The one who deceives his neighbour and says, *"I was joking"* is a madman. Contention ceases where there is no whisperer. He who hates, pretends with his lips, but harbours deceit within. When he speaks pleasantly, do not trust him. Though his hatred is hidden by deceit, his wickedness will be revealed before the congregation.

He who digs a pit will fall into it. He who rolls a stone will have it come back upon him. A lying tongue hates those it crushes, and a flattering mouth works ruin. Do not boast about tomorrow for you do not know what will happen today. Let someone else praise you and not your own mouth, a stranger and not your own lips.

Anger is cruel and overwhelming, but who can stand before jealousy? Better a rebuke revealed than a rebuke concealed. Faithful are the wounds of a friend, and profuse are the kisses of an enemy. To him who is hungry, everything bitter is sweet. A man who wanders from his place is like a bird who wanders from its nest. Oil and perfume make the heart rejoice, as does the pleasantness of a friend's suggestion from the heart.

Do not forsake your friend and your father's friend. Do not go into your brother's house in the day of your trouble. Better a neighbour who is near than a brother who is far away. A prudent man sees evil and hides himself, but the simple go on and are punished. He who blesses his neighbour with a loud voice, rising early in the morning will have it reckoned to him as a curse.

To restrain a contentious woman is like restraining the wind. A constant dripping on a rainy day and a contentious woman are alike. He who watches over a fig tree will eat its fruit. He who protects his master will be honoured. As in water, face answers to face, so the heart of one man answers to another. A man is tested by what he praises. Know thoroughly the condition of your flocks and keep your mind on the herds, for riches are not forever.

The wicked run away when there is no one chasing them, but the righteous are as fearless as a young lion. A poor man who oppresses the weak is like a cloudburst that leaves no nourishment. Those who forsake the Law praise the wicked, but those who keep the Law contend with them. Evil men do not understand justice, but those who seek the Lord understand all about it.

Better is a poor man walking in his integrity, than a perverse double dealer, though he be rich. A companion of gluttons puts his father to shame. He who augments his wealth by interest and increase will gather it for him who is considerate of the poor.

The one who causes the righteous to go astray in an evil way will fall into his own pit. A rich man is wise in his own eyes, but a discerning poor man will see through him. Great is the glory when the righteous rejoice. He who conceals his transgressions will not prosper, but he who confesses and forsakes them will receive mercy. Blessed is the man who is always reverent, but he who hardens his heart will fall into calamity. He who hates covetousness will prolong his days. Whoever walks whole-heartedly will be saved. He who follows worthless pursuits will have plenty of poverty. He who chases wealth shall not escape the penalty.

To show partiality is not good. He whose eye is evil hurries after wealth, but he does not know that he will end up wanting. He who rebukes a man will afterwards find more favour than he who flatters with his tongue.

He who trusts in the Lord will be enriched. He who trusts in his own heart is a fool, but he who walks in wisdom will escape. He who gives to the poor will never lack for anything, and he who hides his eyes will receive many curses. When the wicked perish, the righteous increase. The man who is often reproved but stiffens his neck will suddenly be broken beyond remedy.

He who associates with harlots wastes his substance. The man who flatters his neighbour spreads a net upon his steps. There is a snare in the transgression of an evil man. The righteous man knows the rights of the weak; the wicked man does not understand such knowledge.

Scorners set a city aflame, but wise men turn away anger. Bloodthirsty men hate the man of integrity, but the upright seek his life. A fool gives full vent to his anger, but the wise man, holding back, quiets it. If a ruler listens to false suggestions, all his officials will be wicked. The poor and the oppressor meet, and the Lord gives light to the eyes of both. The king who judges the weak faithfully will have his throne established forever.

The rod and reproof give wisdom, but an undisciplined child causes his mother shame. When the wicked increase, transgression multiplies, but the righteous will observe their fall. Correct your son and he will give you rest and joy to your soul. Happy is he who keeps the Law. There is more hope for a fool than for a man of hasty words. A quick-tempered man stirs up trouble, and a man who gets angry is always wrong.

He who pampers his servant from childhood will afterwards have him for a son. A man's pride will bring him low, but the lowly in spirit obtains honour. The fear of man brings a snare, but whoever trusts in the Lord will be lifted up. Justice due a man comes from the Lord. Every word of God has been proven true. He is a shield to those who take refuge in Him. Add not to His words, lest He reprove you and you be found a liar.

Do not slander a servant to his master lest he curse you, since you are guilty. The eye that mocks a father and scorns to obey a mother will be picked out by the ravens of the valley and eaten by the young vultures. Getting angry will cause you problems. Don't give your strength to women or your ways to what destroy kings, like wine and strong drink, lest you forget what is decreed and pervert the rights of the afflicted. Give strong drink to him who is perishing and wine to the bitter of soul; let him drink and forget his poverty so that he no longer remembers his misery.

Speak up for the dumb, and for the cause of those who are left desolate. Speak up, judge righteously, and defend the rights of the poor and the needy. A wife with strength of character is far more precious than jewels. She will do you good and not harm all the days of her life. Charm is deceitful, and beauty is passing, but a woman who revers the Lord will be praised.

ECCLESIASTES

These are the words of the Preacher (Solomon), son of David, king of Jerusalem.

"Everything is futile; one generation goes, another comes. The sun rises, and it sets. The wind, the sea, the rivers, and the earth have always been there doing the same things and will continue to do the same things forever. Nothing is new under the sun. There is no remembrance of the past or future. I ruled Jerusalem and had plenty of wisdom and knowledge, but all that is like chasing the wind. With more wisdom comes more vexation, and increasing one's knowledge increases one's distress. Having a good time with laughter and amusement is also worthless. What does it accomplish?

"I built houses, planted gardens, vineyards, trees, and parks. I had servants, mistresses, children, and all the treasures possible. Anything I wanted, I got. I was the most powerful man in the world, yet when I look at everything in perspective, they are all worthless like chasing the wind.

"Light is better than darkness. Wisdom is better than folly, but for a wise man, there is no more lasting remembrance than for a fool. Both will die and be forgotten. All the work that I did will be left behind when I die, and someone else will take over, and who knows whether he will be a wise man or a fool. All my work will go to someone who did not work for it. So what does a man get for all his work? It's all emptiness!

"There is nothing better for a man than to eat, drink, and get enjoyment from his work. Everything comes from the Hand of God. Only He can eat with enjoyment. He gives to the man who pleases Him, wisdom, knowledge, and joy, while to the sinner He commits the task of gathering and heaping in order to give it to the one who pleases Him.

"There is a time for everything. So what benefit does the workman get from that which wears himself out? God has made everything beautiful in its time without man finding out how He does it. There is nothing better than to rejoice and do good all through life. If a man eats, drinks, and sees good in all he does, it is God's gift. Everything that God does will remain forever. Nothing can be added or taken from it. He did it so that we should be reverent in His presence. Whatever exists now has been around for a long time, and whatever will exist in the future has also existed long ago. Under the sun, which is the place of judgement, there was wrong; in the place of righteousness, there was wickedness.

"God will judge the righteous and the wicked for there is a time for every purpose and every work. God tests men to see that in themselves, they are but animals. The fate of men and animals is the same. Both have breath and both will die and go to one place, and all will return to dust. "No one knows what comes after, so there is nothing better than for a man to rejoice in his works. That is his position in life.

"All the toil and skill in activities bring envy between a man and his neighbour. The fool folds his hands together and consumes his own flesh. Better is a handful with rest, than both fists full of toil and chasing after the wind. Two are better than one because they gain a good reward for their toil. If they fall, one will help the other. But there will be problems for the one who falls alone, if there is no one to lift him up.

"It is better to be a poor and wise youth than an old and foolish king who no longer knows how to take advice. To be ready to listen is better than to give sacrifice like the fools who do not know when they do wrong. Don't be hasty with your heart and your mouth, and don't allow it to be hasty in uttering the wrong things in front of God.

"When you make a promise to God, don't delay in paying it because He takes no pleasure in fools. It is better not to make any promise at all than to make one and not pay it. You must revere God!

"Don't be surprised if you see the oppression of the poor and the seizure of justice and right because a high official is guarded by a higher one and a much higher one guards over them. The lover of money will not be satisfied with only money, nor the lover of wealth with his gain. Sweet is the sleep of the toiler whether he eats little or much, but the abundance of the rich will not let him sleep. As one comes naked from his mother's womb, so he will return the way he came, and for all his work, he can take nothing with him.

"One should eat and drink and find enjoyment in what one has honestly worked for during one's life, which is given by God, because that is one's lot. Every man to whom God has given riches and wealth and power to enjoy them should do so; it is the gift of God. He will never think of how short his life really is because God keeps his heart occupied in happiness.

"It often happens that a man to whom God has given riches, wealth, and honour will not be given the opportunity to enjoy it, and in the end a stranger will enjoy it. If a man has 100 children and lives many years and his soul is not satisfied with all the good that God has done for him, and what's more he has no burial, then an untimely birth is better off than he. What the eyes see is better than the wanderings of desire.

"A human being cannot contend with God who is stronger than he. The more words you use, the more worthless they are. A good name is better than a good ointment. The day of death is better than the day of birth. It is better to go to the house of mourning than to the house of feasting, because this is the destiny of all men, and the living should take it to heart. Sorrow is better than laughter, because facial sadness makes the heart glad. The heart of the wise is in the house of mourning, but the house of fools is in the house of gaiety.

"It is better to hear the reproof of the wise than to hear the song of fools. It is better to be patient than proud. Don't get offended quickly, because resentment lives in the heart of fools. Wisdom is beneficial, an advantage, and it preserves the lives of those who possess it. In the day of prosperity enjoy life, and in the day of adversity remember that God made both.

"In life, there is the righteous man who perishes in his righteousness, and the wicked man who prolongs his life in his wickedness. Don't be wicked, nor play the fool, or you will die before your time. He who reveres God comes clear of both. There is nobody who does good and never sins. Don't pay attention to everything that people say, lest you hear your servant curse you, and you know well in your heart that you have cursed others. Whoever pleases God will escape trouble, and the sinner will fall into it. Whoever observes the royal orders will experience no harm.

"The heart of the wise man knows time and procedure. For every interest there is a time and a decision, since a person's trouble rests heavily on him. As no one can be master over the wind, so no one can prevail on his day of death. Where no sentence is speedily executed upon the criminal that is where the heart of men is filled with schemes to do evil. All will be well with those who revere God and are in awe of Him. All will not be well with the evil doer, because he does not revere God.

"No one can see himself sleeping therefore no one can discover the work of God. A wise man will work hard and search, but he will never find it. The activities of the righteous and the wise are in the Hand of God, love as well as hate. Man knows nothing of what lies ahead of him. Everything is the same for everybody, one fate for both the righteous and the wicked. Just enjoy yourself with a merry heart, for God has already accepted you and your doings.

"Do whatever you are able to do with all your might because there is neither work, nor invention, nor knowledge, nor wisdom in Hell, towards which you are moving. Wisdom is better than strength, but the poor man's wisdom is despised, and his words are not considered. The words of the wise heard quietly are better than the shouts of a ruler among fools. Wisdom is better than weapons of war, but a lot of good can be destroyed by one sinner. A little folly outweighs an abundance of wisdom. A wise man's heart turns to the right, and a fool's heart turns to the left. A fool lacks sense and lets everybody know that he is a fool.

"If a ruler's temper rises against you, do not resign your position, for composure may remedy serious mistakes. He who digs a pit shall fall into it, and he who breaks through a wall shall be bitten by a serpent. He who removes stones will be hurt by them, and he who splits logs will be endangered by them. Wisdom is an advantage for gaining success. If a snake bites before charming then the charmer's skill does not benefit.

"Man does not know what is to be. Who can tell him what will happen after his lifetime? Through continual neglect, the ceiling sinks and the house leaks because of slack hands. Money brings about everything, so do not curse the rich or the king, even in your thoughts because a bird in the heavens may convey your voice and a winged creature may repeat your words. Cast your bread upon the waters, for you will find it after many days. Divide it into seven or eight portions, for you do not know what trouble there may be on the earth in the future. No one knows the work of God who makes everything.

"In the morning, sow your seed and in the evening, don't be idle because you don't know which of them will prosper. Light is sweet, but also consider the darkness. Take pleasure in your youth, follow the ways of your heart and the sight of your eyes, but be aware that for all these God will call you to account.

"Banish grief from your mind and keep pain from your body because youth and the dawn of life are transitory. In the days of your youth, be mindful of your Creator, before the troubling days come and the years draw near, before you go to your eternal home and the mourners go about in the street. That is when the dust returns to the earth as it was and your spirit returns to God who gave it.

"There is no end to the making of many books, and much study is wearying to the body. Above all, it is every person's duty to revere and love God. Keep His Commandments because He will bring every work into judgement, even everything hidden, whether it be good or bad."

THE SONG OF SOLOMON

There is some controversy over the meaning of this book. The Jews say that the bridegroom represents God and the Shulammite bride, "God's people." Other Christians say that the bridegroom is Christ and the Shulammite bride, the Church.

As the title suggests, it is a love song written by Solomon, which is hard to explain without having to rewrite it in its entirety. It is a short book, so it would be better to find a Bible and read it, as it would have different meanings to different people.

The Outline:

Chapter one is about the mutual admiration of the lovers.
Chapter two is to do with the growth in their love.
Chapter three is the marriage.
Chapter four is the longing of the wife for her absent husband.
Chapter five describes how beautiful the Shulammite bride is.
Chapter six focuses on the wonder of love.

THE BOOK OF ISAIAH

This book is about the vision of Isaiah, the son of Amoz, which he saw concerning Judah and Jerusalem during the reigns of Uzziah, Jotham, Ahaz, and Hezekiah the kings of Judah. This is what the Lord said to Isaiah, "*I have trained and brought up children but they have become rebellious against Me. Israel does not understand and lacks discernment. Even a donkey knows its owner.*"

Isaiah continues by saying that they have forsaken and shown contempt for God and that is why their country is devastated and their cities have been burnt down and plundered by foreigners.

This is what God also told Isaiah: "*What significance are your numerous sacrifices to Me? I am tired of all your offerings and festivals! Your hands are full of blood. Purify yourselves and remove your wickedness from My eyes. Learn to do good! If you become obedient, you will eat the good of the land, but if you refuse and are rebellious, you will die. All sinners will be crushed and those who forsake Me will be annihilated.*"

Isaiah continues by saying that eventually the Lord's House will be established and people will be united and follow God's ways. Weapons will be changed for tools, disputes between nations will be settled, and there will be no more war. Proud men will be brought low, haughty men humbled, and only God will be exalted. All idols will vanish, and sinners will slink away into caves and holes in God's presence. God is about to remove all support and sustenance from Jerusalem and Judah, because their language and deeds are against the Lord, thereby provoking the glorious way He looks at the world.

Because the daughters of Zion are proud, God will expose their secret parts. Instead of a sweet smell, there will be rottenness. A sackcloth, instead of a rich robe. Instead of beauty, a branding mark. Their men will die by the sword, and her gates will mourn and grieve. When everything has been cleansed, the Lord's branch will become beautiful and glorious, and the fruit of the land will be excellent and splendid for the escapees of Israel.

God's vineyard is the House of Israel, and the men of Judah are His cherished planting. He eagerly looked for justice but got bloodshed instead. There will be problems for those joining house to house, those who continually sin, those who call evil good and good evil, those who are champions of drinking wine or taking intoxicants, and those who acquit the guilty for a bribe while taking the rights from the righteous. They have rejected the teachings of God and do not show regard for the deeds of the Lord. God is angry with His people, and He has stretched out His Hand upon them and killed them.

In the year of king Uzziah's death, Isaiah saw God sitting on a throne and His robes filled the Temple. The seraphim were standing above Him and singing, *"Holy, Holy, Holy is the Lord of Hosts, the whole earth is full of His Glory."* One of the seraphim put a hot coal on Isaiah's lips, and all his sins were forgiven. God then sent him to relate to the people about their sufferings until all their cities were ruined.

In the days of Ahaz, the son of Jotham and grandson of Uzziah, the king of Judah, Rezin, the king of Syria, waged war against Jerusalem but could not conquer it. God asked Isaiah to warn Ahaz that the attack would not succeed. God tested Ahaz to make a sign of either Heaven or Hell, but Ahaz refused to test the Lord who then told him about the coming of the Messiah who would be born of a virgin and would be called Immanuel. He would know how to choose between evil and good. Judah would be flooded and submerged because the people had rejected the waters of Shiloah.

God continued by saying that he shouldn't follow the signs of the people because they would stumble and fall, broken, trapped, and taken. Shouldn't the people consult with God instead of necromancers and fortune tellers? Those who don't consult God will be distressed and hungry, in a gloom of anguish and be thrust into darkness. But things will change, and there will be joy when the child is born. He will be called Wonderful, Counsellor, Mighty God, Everlasting Father, and Prince of Peace. All the suffering for the people of Israel and Judah was because they did not turn to God.

Isaiah continues by saying that God's anger has not subsided because they are still godless and wicked. They will continue to be famished, suffer, and eventually be destroyed. For those issuing unrighteous decrees and putting injurious decisions into writing, who will they turn to when the day of visitation and annihilation comes?

Assyria will suffer the same fate as Jerusalem and Samaria when God has finished his work on mount Zion. It will be destroyed by fire and wasting disease. Only then will the survivors of Israel and Judah finally turn back to God. God will judge by what His ears hear and will judge everybody with fairness. The wicked will be killed, and the righteous will become part of Him. God will stretch out His Hand and forgive the righteous. Judah's hostility will be done away with, and all her enemies will be humbled.

On that day, those who are saved will praise and thank God. The day of the Lord will come and destroy everything evil. The sun will be dark, and there will be no light coming from the moon. God will put an end to the arrogant, the proud, and all sinners. The heavens will tremble, and the earth will quake. Babylon will be destroyed, just like Sodom and Gomorrah.

God will then have compassion on Jacob and will still choose Israel. Her people will then prosper, and they will make captives of those who took them captive. They will no longer suffer. The earth will be at ease and quiet, and people will rejoice.

The new Israel will not be recognised from the one in the past, which caused so much havoc and sin. The descendants of Moab (grandson of Lot), however, will continue to suffer, and all their land will be barren. They will cry out in distress, all to no avail. Within three years, the glory of Moab will be brought into contempt, and what remains of it will be small and insignificant.

Damascus will be destroyed. The glory of Jacob will decrease, and only very little of it will remain. Man will turn to God and forget about altars and sun images. Strong cities will be ruined and desolated. Crops will be planted, yet they will vanish, all because they have forgotten God. They should look when a signal is raised on the mountains and listen when a trumpet is blown.

God also told Isaiah that Egyptians will fight each other until they are exhausted, and then they will turn to idols and magicians. A cruel king will rule over them. The sea will dry up, rivers will become polluted, and her people will suffer. She has been led astray by her rulers and princes. She will be terrorised by Judah, and one of her cities will be called the city of destruction. Egyptians will then cry to the Lord's altar, which is situated in the middle of Egypt, because of their oppressors.

God will, however, send a Saviour to deliver them and reveal Himself to them, only then will they finally learn to worship and offer sacrifices to Him. Egyptians will then join Assyrians in serving God, after first being defeated and put into captivity by the Assyrians.

Isaiah then tells of how Babylon will fall. Within a year, all the glory of Kedar will come to an end. (Kedar was the son of Ishmael and the grandson of Abraham.) God will give authority to Eliakim, the son of Hilkiah, and he will become the father to the inhabitants of Jerusalem and to the House of Judah.

Tyre will be forgotten for seventy years, after which God will give everything belonging to her to those who follow Him. All those not following the Lord will have a curse put on their land, and they will not enjoy the good things in life, like music and laughter. Her buildings will be destroyed, and God's Glory will triumph in the end. After destruction, God will make a feast for the people remaining and make everybody happy. People will then recognise God as the true power and praise Him.

Eventually Israel will prosper again. The iniquities of Israel can only be atoned for by God's punishment. All those who sin and scoff will be destroyed. Those who believe in God and repent will be saved. Scoff no more or God will annihilate the whole earth.

Distress will come to Ariel (Jerusalem) in the form of thunder, earthquake, whirlwind, and storms because people only pay lip service but are not really true to God. In the end, the children from the House of Jacob who draw close to God will prosper, and the rest will end up in shame and disgrace.

Those who wait on the Lord will be shown mercy because God is kind, loving, and gracious. Their animals will feed well, their crops will grow plentifully, and all their wounds will be healed. Children of Israel should return to God from whom they so gravely revolted.

Eventually a king will reign in righteousness, princes will rule in justice, and God will make sure everything goes well. The hungry will eat, the blind will see, the deaf will hear, and there will be peace. Anyone who looks unfavourably on evil will live on the heights. His bread will be provided for him, and his water will be guaranteed. God is angry with all nations who sin and will slaughter them. The Lord has a day of retribution and a year of recompense for the cause of Zion. Search and read it out of the Lord's book, and God will come and save you.

There will be a Holy Way, but the unclean or fools will not travel on it. The Lord's ransomed will return to Zion with singing and everlasting joy, whilst sorrow and sadness will disappear.

During Hezekiah's reign, Judah was occupied by Sennacherib the king of Assyria, who sent his intermediaries to meet Eliakim and negotiate their surrender. They told Eliakim not to trust the Egyptians or listen to Hezekiah who was against the Lord. They even offered 2,000 horses and new land to settle, in order to disown Hezekiah.

When he heard it, Hezekiah tore his clothes, put on a sack-cloth, and prayed to God to save them. Isaiah told him that he had done wrong to God and that is why he was in trouble. He would suffer for two years but prosper in the third. The king of Assyria would not attack but would rather go back home and die.

An angel later went and killed 185,000 Assyrians. Sennacherib himself was murdered by his sons. Hezekiah fell ill and was about to die when Isaiah told him to set his house in order and pray to God, which he did, so God lengthened his life by another fifteen years and defended his city for him.

When Hezekiah was sick, Merodach-baladan, the son of Baladan (king of Babylon), came to visit him and sent presents. Hezekiah was so happy that he showed him his whole kingdom, including all his treasures. Isaiah told him that one day he would lose everything to the king of Babylon and even some of his sons would become slave eunuchs in the king of Babylon's palace.

Jerusalem should be happy because God had forgiven all her sins. The Glory of God would be revealed, and they would prosper. Everybody should praise God because He was coming to save the world. God made everything, and whole nations are nothing to Him because His Spirit is all-powerful. Just look around and ask who created everything in this world. God had not neglected Israel but had rather blessed her and made her strong. He would help Israel and all her lands would be fertile, and her people would never lack for anything. They should sing praises to God and glorify His Name because He had helped them. Despite all the bad things that Israel had done, God had still saved and blessed her. They should no longer be afraid. He had redeemed them because they were precious in His sight. There is no other god but the Lord. He is the first and the last. Even the image carvers were confused and put to shame. They should remember that God made them, and He would never forget them.

God one day told Cyrus (the founder of the Persian Empire) that He was the only God, the One who made everything. He would give Cyrus treasures and wealth so that he would know that He was the Lord. He created the heavens, formed the earth, fashioned it, and made it fit for habitation. Only fools carried idols of wood and prayed to gods who could not save. The word of truth comes out of His mouth. Everyone has to bow to Him and glorify His Name. There is no other God like He who announces the end from the beginning and from ancient times, things that have not yet taken place. Virgin daughters of Babylon would suffer from widowhood and loss of childhood because they boasted and thought that they would remain mistresses forever, enjoying life.

God said that He would take vengeance and spare no man because they thought they were so great that they had no equals. Disaster and desolation would come to them. Those who swear by the Name of the Lord and profess the God of Israel, but continue to sin, would suffer. There would be no peace for the wicked.

God then said to Israel, *"You are My servant in whom I will be glorified. When you were in trouble, I helped you. I made you and raised you. I will always protect you. Your people will never be hungry or thirsty. Even though you thought I had forgotten you, I was always there taking care of you and your children. My justice will be a light for your people. My victory will be forever and My salvation will be for all generations.*

"The people saved by Me will return to Zion with singing and everlasting joy. I am the One who comforts you so that you don't fear anybody. You are My people. I have moved the cup that causes you to stagger from your hand. You don't have to drink from it any more. I will give it to those who are oppressing you. Free yourselves from captivity. You sold yourselves for nothing, and without money you will be redeemed.

"You must learn My Name and know that I am the One speaking. Sing and rejoice because the Lord has returned to Zion and redeemed Jerusalem. The God of Israel is your rear-guard. I have carried your sickness and your sorrows. I am your true Maker and the true husband to you women. I will have compassion on you, and I will not be angry with you or rebuke you. No weapon can be used against you anymore. This is your heritage. Look for Me while I may still be found. Call on Me while I am near. Let the unrighteous return to Me, and I will have mercy on them and pardon them. Maintain justice and practise what is right, because My salvation is at hand."

God continued by saying, *"Blessed is the man who observes this, keeps to the Sabbath, does not profane it, and holds fast to My Covenant. You used to worship false idols and you did not remember Me. Was it because I have kept silent for so long that you did not revere Me? All your sins and doings will not benefit you. When you cry, let your idol collection save you, but he who takes refuge in Me will inherit the land and possess My holy mountain*

"I live in the high and holy place. I also live with those who are lowly and contrite in spirit, to restore the spirit of the humble and to revive the heart of the contrite. I was angry for some time because of your sins and your greed, and I destroyed you. I allowed you to go astray, but now I will heal you, guide you, and repay with comfort those who are sorry.

"There is no peace for the wicked. Your gates will be open continually, your enemies will be captured, and all their wealth brought to you. The glory of Lebanon with its trees will come to you. All those who once despised you will crouch at your feet. They will call you the City of the Lord, Zion, and the Holy One of Israel. You will be an everlasting majesty, a joy for many generations. You will drink the milk of the nations and drain the wealth of kings. Instead of brass, I will bring gold, silver, and bronze. Peace will be your governor

*and Justice your ruler. There will be no more violence, deso-
lation, or ruin in your land or your borders. You will call
your walls Salvation and your city gates Thanksgiving. I will
be your everlasting light and your glory.*

*"Your people will be righteous and possess the land for-
ever. I will hasten everything in its proper time, then you will
know that I am the Lord your Saviour and that your Re-
deemer is the Mighty One of Jacob."*

Isaiah then explained that the Spirit of the Lord God was
on him and the Lord anointed him to preach good tidings to
the humble, heal the broken hearted, proclaim liberty to the
captives, comfort and settle the mourners in Zion, and proclaim the year of the Lord's favour and the day of vengeance
of our God.

Finally, the Lord said, *"Heaven is My throne, and the
earth is My footstool. My Hand made everything. I will look
favourably upon the man who is humble, feels crushed in
spirit, and trembles at My word. I am creating new heavens
and a new earth. The past will be forgotten. I am creating in
Jerusalem, an occasion for joy and her people will rejoice."*

THE BOOK OF JEREMIAH

This book is about what Jeremiah, the son of Hilkiah, one of the priests who lived in the territory of Benjamin, said. The Word of the Lord first came to him in the days of Josiah (the son of Amon, the king of Judah) in the thirteenth year of his reign. The Word continued to come during the reigns of Jehoiakim, son of Josiah until the eleventh year of Zedekiah, and until the captivity of Jerusalem.

The Lord said to Jeremiah, *"Now I have put My words in your mouth. Today I have appointed you as the overseer of nations and kingdoms, to root up, to break down, to destroy, to exterminate, to rebuild, and to establish. Calamity will come to Jerusalem because of their evil and for forsaking Me and offering sacrifices to false gods.*

"Tell them everything I shall command you. They will fight against you, but they will not overcome you because I am with you. Go and announce to Israel to return to Me, and I will not be angry with them because I am a merciful God. I will not be angry forever. Only admit your iniquity that you have rebelled against Me, and I will bring you to Zion and give you everything.

"They will call Jerusalem the throne of the Lord, and they will no longer follow their own evil hearts. Judah and Israel will be one and come to the land I gave as an inheritance to their fathers. I am the true God, the living God, and the everlasting king. When I am angry, the earth quakes, and no nation can endure My indignation. The gods who did not make the heavens and the earth will perish."

The Lord also told Jeremiah to tell the people to obey Him and to listen to the words of the Covenant. Anyone who did not do that would be cursed. However, if they did as He wished then their land would be flowing with milk and honey, and all would be well.

The Lord said that He would bring calamity onto the men of Judah for their iniquities. Even if they cried for mercy, He would not listen to them. We would see if their false gods would help them. The young men would die by the sword, their sons and daughters would die by famine, and there would be nothing left of them.

God then told Jeremiah to buy a potters earthen jar and to go to the Benhinnon Valley with some of the elders of the people and proclaim His Message of calamity to the people for not listening to Him and for following false gods. He told Jeremiah to break the jar in order to explain how He would break the people.

When Pashur, the son of Immer the priest who was an overseer in the Lord's house, heard Jeremiah prophesying, he beat Jeremiah and put him in the stocks, releasing him the next day. Jeremiah then said that God would hand over Judah and all her people and treasures to the king of Babylon and he, Pashur, would go into captivity and die. Nebuchadrezzar would kill all his enemies and not spare nor have pity or compassion on them. Anyone who remained in Judah would die.

The Lord told Jeremiah to tell the king of Judah to execute right and justice and to deliver the plundered out of the hand of the oppressor. He should not do wrong or be violent to the immigrant, the fatherless, or the widow, and he should not shed innocent blood. If they really obeyed everything, then kings sitting upon the throne of David, riding in chariots and horses would enter the gates of his house with their servants and their people. But if they didn't obey them then their house would become a ruin.

God stressed that Shallum, the son of Josiah the king of Judah, who reigned instead of his father, would die in exile and never see his land again for going against Him. Nobody will feel sorry for Jehoiakim, the son of Josiah the king of Judah. He will be buried like a donkey, dragged along and thrown out of the gates of Jerusalem.

God then used two baskets of figs, one bad and one good, in order to describe the two types of people in Judah. The good would return to their land and be saved, while the bad like Zedekiah would be cursed and later perish. Judah would be destroyed and be in slavery to the king of Babylon for seventy years. After the seventy years, He would punish the king of Babylon and his nation for their iniquities.

God gave Jeremiah a cup of wine to give to all the nations that He sent him to, in order that they might stagger and be frantic because of the sword that He was sending amongst them.

When Jeremiah gave God's Message to the people, the priests, prophets, and all the people seized him and threatened to kill him. Jeremiah told them to amend their ways, and God would relent and not bring calamity upon them.

Sometime before, a fake prophet called Urijah had also prophesised the destruction of Judah and was chased to Egypt, captured, and put to death by King Jehoiakim. This time, however, they were afraid to touch Jeremiah because they knew that he was a messenger from God.

In the beginning of Zedekiah's (son of Josiah) reign, God told Jeremiah to remind the people that He made the earth, the people, and everything else so He had every right to do as He wanted. He had chosen to put Judah into Nebuchadrezzar's hands. Anyone refusing to serve Him would be destroyed with famine, pestilence, and death.

Whoever served Him would be left alone to till and live peacefully on his land. They should not listen to their priests, prophets, and soothsayers. All the treasures in Judah would be carried to Babylon until the day He remembered to bring them back to their rightful place.

The prophet Hananiah told Jeremiah that God had told him that He would restore Judah's treasures and people back to their land in two years, and break the yoke of the king of Babylon. Hananiah then took the yoke bars from Jeremiah's neck and shattered them to symbolise what God would do to

Nebuchadrezzar. Jeremiah accused Hananiah of using God's Name to lie to the people and make them trust in him. That same year, in the seventh month, Hananiah died.

Jeremiah sent a letter to Jerusalem telling them not to listen to prophets and soothsayers who only wanted to deceive them. He said that God wanted them to build, live, plant, marry, multiply, and seek the welfare of the city. He would fulfil His promise after seventy years. He would then return them to their own country and restore their fortunes. The Lord would punish Shemaiah the Nehelamite for being a false prophet and preaching rebellion against Him.

God told Jeremiah to write everything He told him into a book. He would soon make a new Covenant with Israel after He had saved them. He would then instil His Laws into their hearts. They would be His people, and He would be their God. He would forgive them of all their iniquities. He would restore them, heal them, and reveal to them an abundance of peace and prosperity. God's new name would be, *"Lord of Righteousness."*

When Jerusalem was being attacked by Nebuchadrezzar, God told Jeremiah to tell Zedekiah, the king of Judah, that even though he would be conquered, he would die in peace and not by the sword. But he had to first free all the Hebrew slaves. After freeing them, however, his people recaptured them and enslaved them again. So for disobeying God, his people would be doomed to die by the sword, pestilence, and famine, and their bodies would become food for the birds and the beasts.

During Jehoiakim's reign, God told Jeremiah to write everything He had told him on a scroll. Jeremiah told Baruch the son of Neriah to write everything down according to his dictation. When Baruch read it out to the people, the princes told him and Jeremiah to hide because they would have to tell the king what had been written. On showing the king the scroll, he took it, cut it up, and threw it into the fire. He then ordered the arrest of Baruch and Jeremiah.

God told Jeremiah to write another scroll, which he again dictated to Baruch. He promised to punish Jehoiakim, his offspring, and his servants for their iniquity.

During Zedekiah's reign, the Chaldean (Babylonian) army had almost finished Jerusalem but retreated on seeing the Egyptians. Jeremiah was arrested, accused of desertion, and thrown into jail. He was later put under house arrest, after he had delivered God's Message to Zedekiah that he would be conquered by Nebuchadrezzar.

The princes tried to kill Jeremiah by putting him into a cistern. Luckily, a eunuch called Ebedmelech told Zedekiah, who had him rescued back to his house arrest.

Jeremiah told Zedekiah that if he did not surrender to the Chaldeans, then he and his city would be destroyed, but if he surrendered, his life would be spared. Jeremiah did not, however, tell the princes what he and Zedekiah had discussed. He remained under house arrest until Jerusalem was taken.

Zedekiah and the princes were captured, and his sons were killed in front of him. All the princes and nobles were killed. Zedekiah was blinded and taken in chains to Babylon.

The walls of Jerusalem were broken, and all the houses were destroyed by fire. The poor were left in Judah and given land to live and work on. Jeremiah was rescued and taken home. He was given food and a present, and then he was set free. He lived among the people of Judah.

Gedaliah was made governor of Judah by Nebuchadrezzar. He told the people to feel free and support the king of Babylon. Only the poorest were not taken into captivity and exile. Jews came from all over to live in the land of Judah.

When told that Ishmael (one of the chief officers of Baalis, the king of the Ammonites) was after him to kill him, Gedaliah did not believe it and was killed as he ate with Ishmael, who also killed all his guards. He had been sent by Baalis. Ishmael also slaughtered eighty men who had come to bring gifts to the House of the Lord and threw all the bodies into a cistern. He took the rest of the people prisoner and escaped back to the Ammonites after being chased by Johannan (the captain of Gedaliah's men) and his men, who rescued the people from him and brought them back.

The people, however, later left and went to live near Bethlehem because they were afraid of what the Chaldeans would do to them because of Gedaliah's murder. They asked Jeremiah to pray to God for them. God told him to tell them to stay in Jerusalem and not to be afraid of the king of Babylon. If, however, they returned to Egypt, they would be killed by the sword, famine, and pestilence. They did not listen to Jeremiah and went to Egypt where they continued to burn incense to the queen of heaven and pray to false gods.

God told Jeremiah that Egypt would soon be conquered by Nebuchadrezzar. The people of Moab (descendants of Lot) would also be destroyed for having false gods. The Ammonites would suffer the same fate except that with them, God would restore their fortunes. Edom would also be destroyed and become a horror story. Damascus would be destroyed by fire. Kedar and Elam would also be destroyed, but God would restore the fortunes of Elam. The Chaldeans would one day be destroyed by a nation from the North. Babylon would be so desolated that nothing would be able to live on it. In the end, however, Judah would be pardoned for her sins.

THE LAMENTATIONS OF JEREMIAH

The author of this book is not stated, but it is ascribed to Jeremiah.

The book laments the siege and destruction of Jerusalem and sorrows over the sufferings of the inhabitants during this time. It makes a poignant confession of sin on behalf of the people and their leaders, acknowledges the complete submission to the Divine Will, and prays that once again God will favour and restore His people.

Five poems make up the five chapters. Basically, they tell you that God is good to those who wait for Him and to the soul that looks for Him. It is good if one hopes and quietly waits for God's salvation. One should be prepared to suffer in one's youth. God would never keep away from someone forever because He does not willingly make people suffer.

THE BOOK OF EZEKIEL

Ezekiel the priest, son of Buzi, had a vision of God in the land of the Chaldeans during Jehoiachin's exile. God told him to eat a scroll with words written on it and then go back to the House of Israel and speak to them because they had become stubborn and rebellious. God told him to warn the sinners to change from their evil ways in order to save their souls. Those who changed would be saved, and those who didn't would die with their iniquities.

He was told to lie on an iron plate on his left side for 390 days in order to carry their iniquity. This would be equal to the number of years of her punishment. Then he had to lie for 40 days on his right side in order to take on the punishment of Judah, also equal to the number of years of her punishment.

He should then face Jerusalem and prophesy against it. Because she had been rebellious, a third of Jerusalem would die of pestilence, a third by the sword, and a third would be scattered to the wind. Fathers would eat their sons, and sons would eat their fathers. Jerusalem would be desolated and hated by the nations around her and by anyone who went anywhere near her. God would abolish her high places and demolish her altars and idols. The people who had been killed would lie amongst the living, and then they would recognise that He was the Lord. Nothing could save them from God's anger. They would keep on having disasters.

In another vision, God showed Ezekiel all the evil things that the people were doing, like praying to false gods. God sent a man to put a mark on the foreheads of those who were against the evil doers and then sent others to kill the rest of them, which they did. Ezekiel tried to plead for them but to no avail because God was too angry with them.

Ezekiel told a group that God was out to destroy them for their iniquities. He would scatter all the people to different lands but would one day give them back their land after he had removed all traces of their sins. He would give them a new heart of flesh and not one of stone as they then had, in order that they might follow his statutes and obey only Him. They would be His people, and He would be their God.

God told Ezekiel to pack his belongings and go into exile. If the people asked him where he was going, he was to tell them he was a symbol for them, and soon they would also go into exile and captivity. But God said He would leave a few survivors to tell the story.

Ezekiel told the elders of Israel that they should repent and turn away from their idols or God would destroy them. God also said that Jerusalem would bear the consequences of their abominations, but He would afterwards forgive her and establish His Covenant with her, and she would know that He was truly the Lord.

All souls belong to Him, and it is the person who sins who will die. If a man is righteous and does what is lawful and fair; if he does not eat on mountains nor worship idols; if he does not seduce his neighbour's wife nor approach a woman in her period of uncleanness; if he does not oppress anybody but rather restores a debtor to his pledge; if he commits no robbery but shares his food with the hungry and clothes the naked with a robe; if he does not lend money on usury nor take a profit; if he does not commit crime, practices strict justice between man and man; if he follows His statutes and is careful to observe His ordinances to always deal truthfully; in short, if such a man does what is right, he will surely live. But anyone who commits evils will die, and his blood will be on himself.

If a son does not follow his father's iniquities, he will live and not be punished for his father's sins. If a wicked man turns away from the sins which he has committed and follows God's statutes, he will surely live and not die. None of his past transgressions will be remembered against him. God has no pleasure in the death of the wicked, but rather the sinner should turn from his wicked ways and live. If a righteous man changes from doing the right thing and commits iniquity, then none of his righteous deeds will be remembered, and he will die because of his unfaithfulness and the sins he has committed.

The people of Israel had committed serious abominations and had forgotten God. Everyone was bent on shedding blood. Father and mother were treated with contempt by their children. The foreigner suffered extortion amongst them, while the widow and the orphan were oppressed. They had despised God's holy things and profaned His Sabbaths. They accused each other falsely in order to shed blood. They ate on the high places and committed lewdness amongst each other. There were those who uncovered their father's nakedness and those who humbled women who were unclean from their impurity. Some committed abominations with their neighbour's wives, lewdly defiled their daughters-in-law, and humbled their own sisters. The men took bribes in order to shed blood, exacted usury and interest, and extorted their neighbours. Because of all that, God would destroy them without mercy. The priests violated God's Law and profaned His holy things, so He would also destroy them.

The Israelites would be attacked by the Babylonians and Chaldeans, who would kill all of them and put an end to their harlotry. They would be delivered into the hands of their enemies, who would take everything that they had. Because the Ammonites rejoiced at the plight of the Israelites, they would also be destroyed by people from the East. Sidon, Moab, Seir, and Edom would suffer the same fate. The Philistines would be destroyed for wreaking malicious revenge on the Israelites.

Nebuchadrezzar, the king of Babylon, would come and destroy Tyre, plundering her wealth and leaving her desolate. She used to be a city of great wealth and prosperity but would be destroyed for going against God. Egypt would also be desolated by Nebuchadrezzar for not recognising God. It would remain uninhabited for forty years, after which she would be restored to her lands. She would, however, be weak and insignificant and would never rise again over other nations.

The day of the Lord would come when Egypt, Ethiopia, Put, Lud, Arabians, Lybians, and all those in league with them would be destroyed. Mount Seir would also be desolated, and her cities destroyed for perpetuating enmity towards the children of Israel. Because Israel was guilty of blood, blood would pursue her, but because of her humiliation and sufferings at the hands of her enemies, God would restore her again to prosperity, and then she would have faith in Him. He would give her a new spirit, and she would observe His ordinances. She would then remember her past abominations and iniquities and be ashamed.

God then showed Ezekiel a miracle by bringing life to some bones lying down in a valley. He then told Ezekiel that He would unite all the Israelites back to their own land and make them all one nation. They would then obey His Commandments. The land of Gog, Meshech, and Tubal would also be destroyed for going against God.

God gave Ezekiel a man who showed him how God's new Temple and its measurements would be made. God then explained that it would be a holy place, and Israel would no longer defile His Holy Name. She would be ashamed of all her iniquities.

God told Ezekiel to tell the priests that on the day the altar was built, they were to offer burnt offerings to Him every day for seven days, make atonement for the altar, and purify and cleanse it, in order to consecrate it. No uncircumcised man would be allowed to enter His Sanctuary.

The Levites were to minister the Temple as guards, which was their punishment for straying from God. But the Levitical priests, the sons of Zadok who kept charge of His Sanctuary when the children of Israel went against Him, were allowed to enter His Sanctuary. Those who entered had to keep His rules and regulations.

God told Ezekiel everything that the priests and the people had to do concerning the Temple, including sacrifices and burnt offerings. God then showed him the tribal boundaries, which would be divided among the twelve tribes of Israel. The tribes were Dan, Asher, Naphtali, Manasseh, Ephraim, Reuben, Judah, Benjamin, Simeon, Issachar, Zebulun, and Gad. The city was to be called *"The Lord Is There."*

THE BOOK OF DANIEL

In the third year of Jehoiakim, the king of Judah's reign, Nebuchadrezzar laid siege to Jerusalem and captured him and all his treasures. He then ordered the eunuch Ashpenaz to train some Israelites to serve him. They were Daniel, Hananiah, Mishael, and Azariah who were renamed Belteshazzar, Shadrach, Meshach, and Abednego by the eunuch.

Daniel and the rest did not want to eat the royal menu, so they begged the eunuch to eat only vegetables and drink water so that they could be later compared with the ones eating the meat and drinking the wine of the royal menu. After ten days, they looked healthier and in better condition, so they were excused from eating the royal menu.

God gave them understanding in literature and science while Daniel gained insight in every vision and dream. They all joined the king's personal service.

One day, Nebuchadrezzar had a disturbing dream, and because the wise men and magicians could not interpret it, he told his guards to kill all of them. God revealed the answer to Daniel in a dream, and he went and explained it to the king who was so grateful, he bowed before Daniel, gave him honours and gifts, and appointed him chief governor over all the wise men of Babylon, thereby saving their lives. Shadrach, Meshach, and Abednego were put in charge of all business in Babylon.

When they refused to worship the king's gold statue, they were thrown into a fire, but they survived, thereby convincing the king that there was only one God, Whom he decreed everybody should worship.

Nebuchadrezzar had another dream, which was interpreted by Daniel that he would lose his kingdom. Daniel advised him to stop sinning and show pity to the oppressed and perhaps God would spare him. But at the end of twelve months, Nebuchadrezzar was driven out of his kingdom and lived with the animals in the fields for seven years. At the end of this, he recognised and praised God and was re-established in his kingdom.

During Belshazzar's (Nebuchadrezzar's grandson) reign, he ordered that his consorts, concubines, and the rest of his royal household eat and drink from the gold and silver utensils from God's Temple. During the feast, a hand came on the wall and wrote a message. In his fear, Belshazzar promised riches to whoever could interpret the writing. All the magicians and wise men failed, so Daniel was brought in.

He explained how God had taught his grandfather Nebuchadrezzar a lesson for not respecting Him, and God would do the same to him if he did not stop following false gods. He should humble himself to God who had given him life and riches. The writing was "*Mene, Mene, Tekel, Upharsin,*" which meant that God had numbered the days of his kingdom and had brought it to an end. He had been weighed on the scales of judgement and found wanting. His kingdom had been divided and given to the Medes and the Persians.

Daniel was promoted to third in the ruling hierarchy of the kingdom.

Belshazzar was later killed, and Darius the Mede took over the kingdom. He appointed governors for his kingdom, of which Daniel established himself as the best. The others were jealous and made Darius sign a decree that whoever prayed to any god within thirty days should be put into a den of lions.

Daniel was caught praying to God, and the king was forced to put him into a den of lions. He was greatly disturbed and went the next morning to the den and found Daniel alive. The king was so overjoyed that he ordered all the detractors, their wives, and children to be put in a den of lions, and they were torn to pieces. He then made a decree that everybody had to worship the true God of Daniel.

Daniel had another dream concerning four animals, which were interpreted as four kingdoms. The fourth would eventually take over the rest. The animals had ten horns out of which would arise ten kings. After this would come one king who would be different and go against God. His kingdom would be taken from him and destroyed forever. The greatness of the kingdoms under Heaven would be given to the people of the saints of God. The kingdoms would be everlasting, and all the dominions would serve and obey them.

Daniel had another dream, which was explained to him by the angel Gabriel. Four kingdoms would develop from the kingdom of Media. A king would emerge and bring ruin, destroying his opponents. He would then be broken. This dream came to Daniel in the third year of Belshazzar's reign.

In the first year of Darius' reign, Daniel found out from the scriptures that Jerusalem would lie desolate for seventy years, and he prayed to God, asking for forgiveness. All the punishment falling on Israel was because she had sinned and gone against God. Gabriel came to Daniel and predicted the Coming of the Messiah who would be killed after sixty-two weeks, even though there was nothing against Him. The city would be destroyed by a prince who was to come. There would be warfare and ruins before finally everything would be desolated.

Daniel had another vision in the third year of Cyrus' (the king of Persia) reign where he was strengthened by an angel and told about the coming of the prince of Greece. The angel also told him that he would convey to him what was recorded in the Book of Truth concerning the future.

In the first year of Darius' reign, Daniel again had a dream, which told him that three more kings would rise up in Persia, and the fourth would be richer than they. He would fight against Greece. Another king would go against God, and his kingdom would be broken. There would be an alliance between North and South, which would later be broken by bloody conflicts. The king of the North would win and become arrogant, thereby losing his kingdom and his life. One of the chief princes called Michael would stand up and defend the children of Israel.

HOSEA

God's Message came to Hosea in the reigns of Uzziah, Jotham, Ahaz, and Hezekiah, the kings of Judah. God told Hosea to marry a harlot, and he chose one called Gomer who bore him two sons, Jezreel and Not-my-people, and a daughter called "Unloved" in order to show His displeasure to Israel, whom He had promised never to show pity for, although He had at one time promised to spare Judah.

God said that He would make Israel suffer until they turned to Him. The priests of Israel condoned immorality, and Israel's sin would be punished unless she repented. Her sin was thorough, but her repentance was only half-hearted. There was inner depravity and outward decay, and what's more, she never turned to Him for anything even though He had trained and made her strong. Her judgement would soon come followed by her punishment of calamity and destruction.

God then said that He would pursue Israel with love. He would bring her back home because, although Ephraim had surrounded Him with lies and Israel with deceit, Judah still acknowledged Him and was faithful to the Holy One. Samaria, however, had to bear her guilt because she had rebelled against Him. She would fall by the sword, her children would be dashed to pieces, and her pregnant women ripped open. Israel should come back to Him, and He would forgive, heal, restore, and love her. Whoever was wise would understand that His ways were right, and transgressors would stumble in their sins.

JOEL

God told Joel, the son of Pethuel, about the locust plague and how it would be removed. He also told him about the coming of the Lord in the near future. Fire would destroy everything. People would run away in fear and anguish. The earth would quake, and the heavens would tremble. The sun and the moon would be darkened, while the stars would lose their brightness. The day of the Lord would be terrible. No one could withstand it.

Everybody should repent, and the priests should ask for forgiveness. He was merciful and compassionate so He would spare them. He would restore them and make them prosper in the future. He would pour out His Spirit on everybody. Those who called upon the Name of the Lord would be saved. He would judge everybody and restore the fortunes of Israel.

AMOS

This book is about what Amos, a shepherd from Tekoa, in the reign of Uzziah, the king of Judah, saw and what he said. He indicted Israel, Judah, and other foreign nations for going against God. He would destroy Damascus, Gaza, Hazael, Syria, Ashod, Ashkelon, Ekon, and the Philistines. Tyre, Ammon, and Rabbah would also be punished. Moab, Israel, and Judah would suffer the same fate.

He then condemned Samaria for her wickedness, that despite all the good God had done for her, she had still not come to Him. He had even given her warnings of drought, pestilence, and death, all to no avail. Amos told her to seek the Lord so that there would still be hope for her, otherwise He would turn against her.

God then told Amos how He was going to destroy Israel with locusts and fire.

Amaziah, the priest of Bethel, told Jeroboam, the king of Israel, that Amos was conspiring against him, because Amos had stated that Jeroboam would die by the sword and Israel would go into captivity away from her own land. Amaziah told Amos to go to Judah and prophesy there. Amos reiterated that tragedy would also fall on him.

God showed Amos a basket of fruit saying that the end had come for Israel. No one would escape, although He promised restoration and prosperity.

OBADIAH

This book is about the vision that Obadiah had concerning the destruction of Edom by God.

God would destroy Edom because of her violence against Judah. All the wise men from Edom would die, and the strong men would be filled with terror. The day of the Lord was near, that is when all the bad things they had done would come back on to them.

Mount Zion, however, would be an escape and a sanctuary, and the House of Jacob would be restored. She would take possession of her heritage and retake the countries that had conquered her. Esau would be repossessed and so would the plain of the Philistines, Gilead, and the fields of Ephraim and Samaria.

JONAH

God asked Jonah, the son of Amittai, to go to the city of Nineveh and preach against her. But Jonah ran away to Tarshish and boarded a ship. God caused a storm and almost sunk the ship. On realizing that Jonah was the cause, the sailors threw him overboard, and the storm stopped. Jonah was swallowed by a big fish and stayed in its stomach for three days and nights. He prayed to God asking for forgiveness, and the fish vomited him onto dry land.

God again told him to go to Nineveh and preach against her. Jonah went and told them that their city would be destroyed in forty days. The king ordered everyone to wear sackcloth, turn from their evil ways, and pray to God for forgiveness, which they did. So God relented and spared them of their punishment.

Jonah was angry and asked God to kill him, but God protected him by putting a gourd over him. The next day, a cut worm destroyed the gourd, and the sun beat upon Jonah's head, making him faint. Jonah was angry, and God told him that he should not have been angry because he did not even work for the gourd and therefore did not have the power to save or destroy it. This made Jonah appreciate how God had felt about Nineveh who did not know the difference between right and wrong.

MICAH

In the days of Jotham, Ahaz, and Hezekiah, the kings of Judah, God told Micah of Moresheth what would happen to Samaria and Jerusalem. They would be destroyed because of the sins of Israel and Judah. He would, however, forgive and bless them. There would be no more war, and they would all come back into His fold. A new ruler of Israel would come out of Bethlehem, who would be blessed by Him, bring peace, and become great. He would deliver the Israelites from the Assyrians.

On that day, God would destroy all the soothsayers, sorcerers, idols, fortifications, and graven images. He would destroy the cities that did not fall in line. They would eat but would not be satisfied. There would be no harvest, and nothing would go right for them, because they insisted on doing evil things.

Micah then said that he would always have faith and wait on the Lord. He would bear God's indignation because he knew that he had sinned.

God said that He would forgive them and rebuild everything if only they humbled themselves and repented. He would then show mercy and forget the past sins.

NAHUM

This was the vision of Nahum of Elkosh.

The Lord is a jealous God, a Lord of retribution and indignation. He takes full vengeance upon His adversaries. He is slow to anger, great in power, and will not acquit the guilty. He is good and is a stronghold in the day of trouble. He knows who commits themselves to Him. He will destroy all those who go against Him and pursue His enemies into darkness. Whatever is plotted against God will be brought to nothing.

This book predicts the downfall of Nineveh, the capital of Assyria. The Lord would destroy everything in the city, because they had gone against Him and sinned. There would be no escape for anybody.

HABAKKUK

This is the vision of Habakkuk the prophet. He was worried that the Jews who were so sinful were not being punished. God told him that the proud Chaldeans would themselves be punished for doing excessive damage to the Jews.
Habakkuk then prayed to God, praising His great power that destroys the ungodly.

ZEPHANIAH

Zephaniah had a vision during the reign of Josiah, the son of Amon, king of Judah. God said that He would completely destroy Judah and all the people of Jerusalem because of their iniquities and praying to false gods. He would punish the princes, spoil their crops, and destroy their houses. Before He destroyed everybody, they should humble themselves, do the right things, and He may forgive them.

Gaza, Ashdad, and Ekron would be destroyed. So would the Canaanites, Cherethites, and the Philistines. Nobody would be left. Moab, Ammon, Assyria, and Ethiopia would also be destroyed. Nineveh would become a desert.

On that day, the people would be ashamed for not following God. The proud and exultant ones would be killed, while those who were poor and humble would be spared. They would take refuge in God who would then restore them and their lands and make them rejoice in Him and prosper.

HAGGAI

In the second year of King Darius' reign, Haggai got a Message from God telling him to rebuild God's Temple after an earlier Message had come from God through Haggai's ministry to Zerubbabel (who was then the governor of Judah) and Joshua (the high priest) that it was not yet time to build it. God promised to supervise it and be glorified by it.

He told them to have faith in Him and be strong because He was with them. In the past, they had gone against Him, but He would forgive them. He had chosen to spare Zerubbabel after everyone else had been destroyed.

ZECHARIAH

Zechariah the prophet got a Message from God in the second year of Darius' reign. God wanted the Israelites to come back to him and not behave like their forefathers had done. They were now dead, but God's decrees had survived.

Zechariah then had a vision of a man riding a red horse, which was interpreted by an angel as them patrolling the earth. The angel begged God to have compassion on Jerusalem. God said that He was not happy with the Jews, and the Gentiles had only helped to worsen the disaster. God then said He would forgive Jerusalem and build His house there. He would let her prosper, and she would fall in line with Him.

Zechariah's next vision of four craftsmen was interpreted by an angel as those coming to scatter and rout the bad people of Judah.

The next vision of a measuring line was interpreted as being used to measure the length and width of Jerusalem.

In another vision, Zechariah saw Joshua (the high priest) as an adversary. He was dressed in dirty clothes, which were interpreted as punishment for not following God. But if he were to change, God would give him everything.

Zechariah saw a gold lampstand with a bowl with seven lights and seven ducts on top of it. Two olive trees were also on it. It was interpreted as a message to Zerubbabel telling him that things were not done by might and power, but only by God. The seven lights were God's eyes travelling through the earth. The two olive trees were the anointed two who were standing by God.

The vision of a flying scroll was interpreted as the judgement that the earth was going to face.

The vision of a bushel measure was interpreted as a woman of wickedness.

A vision of four chariots was interpreted as the four winds of Heaven.

God said that Joshua (the high priest) was His anointed one to rule and build His Temple.

Another vision came to Zechariah in which God told Jerusalem to change and not sin, and He would forgive them and make them prosper. He would, however, destroy Tyre, Ashkelon, Gaza, Ekron, Ashdod, and Philistia.

With Jerusalem, her king would come, righteous and victorious, humble and riding on a donkey. She would once again be saved, made mighty and prosper, because God loved her. He was their God, and they will rejoice in His Name.

A day of the Lord would come, however, when Jerusalem would be captured, plundered, her women raped, and half the city would go into captivity. God would then wage war on all the nations who had sinned.

On that day, there would be no light, and it would be cold and freezing. All the nations who went against Jerusalem would now respect her and go there to worship the King. Whoever did not go would experience drought, plague, and death. He would destroy all their idols, and a fountain would clean them from all their sins.

MALACHI

Malachi was told by God to tell Israel that He was angry with her, especially the priests for not respecting Him by offering blind animals for sacrifice and bringing polluted food to the altar. He would never accept their offerings unless they first made Him happy. If they did not obey Him and give glory to His Name, He would send a curse on them and destroy them and their offspring.

Malachi continued by saying that they all had one Father. One God created everybody, so he did not understand why they were all so faithless to one another and profaned God's Covenant. God would send His Messenger of the Covenant who would cleanse Israel, and she would return to Him.

God would first send Elijah to give everybody a last chance to turn their hearts to each other, and then the day of the Lord would come when all evil doers would perish. Only those who revered His Name would survive, crush the wicked, and prosper.

THE NEW TESTAMENT

THE GOSPEL ACCORDING TO MATTHEW

There were fourteen generations from Abraham to David, fourteen generations from David to the Babylonian exile, and fourteen generations from the Babylonian exile until the Christ.

When Joseph, who was engaged to Mary, found that she had a pregnancy that was not his, he wanted to break off the relationship quietly, but an angel told him to take her as a wife because she was to give birth to a child from the Holy Spirit. He was to call Him Jesus. He was going to save His people from their sins. God had already prophesied this through His prophets.

When Jesus was born in Bethlehem in Judea in the reign of King Herod, wise men came to Jerusalem from the east, following a star and inquiring about him. Herod was disturbed and told the wise men to find Jesus so that he too might worship Him. The wise men found Jesus and brought Him gifts of gold, frankincense, and myrrh. They were warned by God in a dream not to return to Herod.

An angel came to Joseph in a dream and warned him to take his family and escape to Egypt. Herod was annoyed and ordered every male child less than two years of age to be killed. When Herod died, the angel told Joseph to return with his family to Israel, but they went instead to Nazareth in the Galilean region because they heard Archelaus had succeeded his father, Herod.

One day, John the Baptist, dressed in rough clothes woven in camel hair, was busy baptising people in the Jordan River and telling them to confess their sins when Jesus came to him to be baptised. As soon as Jesus was baptised, the heavens opened, the Spirit of God came on to Him, and a voice from Heaven said, *"This is My Beloved Son in whom I am well pleased."*

Jesus was then led by the Spirit to the desert where He fasted for forty days and nights. The devil tempted Jesus, asking Him to turn stones into bread, urging Him to jump from a height, and promising Him all the kingdoms of the world, if He would only give him recognition. Jesus refused, and the devil left Him.

When Jesus heard that John the Baptist had been arrested, He left Nazareth and went to live in Capernaum by the sea where He started preaching and telling people to repent because the Kingdom of Heaven was coming. He met two brothers, Simon who was also called Peter, and his brother Andrew, fishing. He told them He would make them fishers of men, and they abandoned their nets and followed Him. James and his brother John also left their boat and their father to follow Jesus.

Jesus was healing and preaching, and His Name spread all over Syria. Everybody who came to Him was healed. He was followed by great crowds wherever He went. Jesus went up on to the hill and taught His disciples the *"Beatitudes,"* which were qualities expected of them. Jesus said that He had not come to annul the law or the prophets but to complete them. He told them never to get angry, insult, or bear a grudge against anybody. Anyone who even looks lustfully at a woman has in his heart already committed adultery with her. Do not marry a divorced woman or swear falsely but always perform your oaths to God. Always give to beggars and never refuse a borrower. Love your neighbour and also your enemies. All charities and gifts should be given in secret because your reward will be in Heaven.

You should always pray in secret and not heap up empty phrases because God will always listen to you. Jesus then taught them how to pray saying "Our Father" (The Lord's Prayer) as the acceptable form of prayer. He taught them how to fast and to respect and love God above everything because He made everything and will always look after them.

Never worry about tomorrow because it will have its own problems. Don't pass judgement because that is the same way God will judge you. Ask and it will be given to you. Look for something and you will find it. Knock and it will be opened to you. Do for others what you would like to be done for you. Beware of false prophets who are wolves in sheep's clothing. A good tree cannot bear bad fruit and vice versa. Anyone who follows God's Laws will be blessed, and those who don't are like fools who will never prosper.

The crowds following Jesus watched Him heal a leper and tell him not to tell anyone but rather offer a gift to his priest. In Capernaum He then healed a centurion's son who was paralysed. He later cured Peter's mother-in-law who was bedridden with fever. He cast out evil spirits from many demoniacs and healed all those who had diseases. When one of His disciples asked Him permission to go and bury his father, Jesus told him to follow Him and to let the dead bury the dead.

One day, they were on a ship when violent storms came and frightened His disciples. Jesus rebuked them for having so little faith and calmed the storms. They wondered what kind of man He was, because even the winds and waves obeyed Him!

When they reached the land of the Gadarenes, Jesus cured two demoniacs by sending the demons that were in them into a herd of pigs, which then rushed down a precipice into the sea and drowned. The former demoniacs went to town and told everyone, so the townspeople begged Jesus to move out of their district. He returned to Galilee.

After letting a paralysed man on a couch walk, the crowds were so awed, they praised God. Jesus then told Matthew, a tax collector, to leave his job and follow Him. When the Pharisees asked why He was sitting with sinners and tax collectors, Jesus replied that the healthy did not need a physician. He did not come to call the righteous to repentance, but the sinners. Jesus lectured them with proverbs and advice.

A woman who suffered from haemorrhaging came up behind Jesus and touched His robe and was healed because of her faith. Jesus brought a dead girl to life at a ruler's house.

He then made two blind men see and told them not to tell anyone, but they went and spread His fame all over the region. Jesus then made a dumb man speak and travelled all over the towns and villages, teaching in their synagogues, and healing every disease and illness.

Jesus gave His disciples, Simon Peter and his brother Andrew, James and his brother John, Philip, Bartholomew, Thomas, Matthew, James (Son of Alphaeus), Thaddaeus, Simon (the Zealot), and Judas Iscariot power to heal the sick and to preach in His Name, but they were never to take any reward for what they did. They should be kind, tactful, and wary of enemies who may punish them, but they should never show fear because God would protect them. Anyone who did not love Him or was not prepared to die for Him was not worthy to follow Him. Whoever lost his life because of Him would find it again.

When John the Baptist, who was in prison, heard about Jesus, he asked his own disciples to inquire of Jesus if He were truly the Coming One. Jesus told them to tell him all that He had done to heal people. Jesus preached that though John the Baptist was great, he was small compared to those in the Kingdom of Heaven. Jesus then reproached the towns in which He had done most of His miracles, for not repenting. He explained to them that only God understood His Son and only the Son understood God.

On one Sabbath, the Pharisees reprimanded Jesus when they saw His disciples plucking heads of grain to eat because they were hungry. When asked if it was lawful to heal on the Sabbath, Jesus replied that it was always lawful to do good on the Sabbath and promptly healed a paralysed man in the synagogue. It was then that the Pharisees started their plan to destroy Him, and Jesus, knowing this, left the place followed by many who He continued healing.

Jesus cured a blind and dumb demoniac, and the Pharisees were annoyed that He was using Beelzebul, the ruler of demons, to expel demons. Jesus explained that to rob a strong man's house, one had first to subdue the man, and then the rest would be easy. Whoever was not with Him was against Him.

All sins and slanders are forgivable for men except slanders about the Spirit. Anything that man does will be answerable on Judgement Day. When asked for proof by the Pharisees, Jesus answered that only wicked men look for proof and the only proof would come from Jonah who spent three days in a fish's stomach.

Something greater than both Jonah and Solomon is here. An unclean spirit will never settle and find peace. When told that His mother and brothers wanted to talk to Him, Jesus replied that everybody who obeyed God's will was His brother, mother and sister.

Jesus on the same day told the parable of the sower. A sower went out to sow. Some of the seeds fell on the pathway where birds easily plucked them up. Others fell on shallow soil over rock, and what grew was scorched by the sun because there were no deep roots. Some fell among thorns, and the thorns grew up and choked them. The rest fell on good soil and bore a good crop.

Asked why He spoke in parables, Jesus replied that whoever has, will receive plenty, and whoever has not, will be deprived of whatever he has. Many people in the past were not lucky enough to be seeing what they were now witnessing. The parable of the sower means that anyone who hears the Message of God and does not understand it will lose everything he has worked for. This is represented by the seed sown on the path. Those that fell on the rocky soil refer to the one who hears the Word and accepts it gladly, but it does not stick with him and does not last, because the Message brings him trouble and persecution, and so he turns away from it. Those that fell on thorns refer to one who listens to the Message but enjoyment of wealth and worldly cares choke the Word, and it becomes unproductive. But what was sown on good ground refers to the one who listens and understands the Message. He bears fruit and yields a profit. The Kingdom of Heaven was like a field of good grain and weeds. When they have sprouted and grown and have grain ready for harvest, the good will be separated from the weeds.

The Kingdom of Heaven is like a mustard seed. It is the smallest of all seeds that when grown up becomes a very large bush to which birds come and roost on its branches. The Kingdom of Heaven is like yeast that a woman took and buried in a bushel of flour until it was all raised.

The parable of the weeds explains that the Son of Man is the sower of the good seed. The field is the world. The good seeds are the children of the Kingdom, and the bad seeds are the evil children of the devil who sowed the weeds. The reapers are the angels. The bad will be picked out and burnt. The Kingdom of Heaven is like a good pearl, a treasure, and a net full of fish. All that is good will remain, and the bad will be destroyed. After Jesus finished, He went to His home town but refused to perform miracles there because of the disbelief of the people.

At that time, Herod had imprisoned John the Baptist because John had told him that he was not allowed to marry Heroidas, his brother's wife. Her daughter asked for John's head when asked by Herod to choose anything she wanted as a present on Herod's birthday. John's head was cut off and presented to her. John's disciples went and told Jesus who continued healing and fed at least five thousand people with five loaves and two fishes. He then dismissed the crowd and went on to a hill to pray.

When the disciples went out to the sea and had problems with the waves, Jesus came to them while walking on the water. Jesus accused Peter of having too little faith when he sank as he tried to walk on the water towards Him. Jesus held him up, and the disciples said, "*Truly You are the Son of God.*"

They sailed to Gennesaret where Jesus continued healing. He accused the Pharisees of being hypocrites and going against God's word with their traditions. Jesus explained that whatever goes into a man's mouth will be digested and purged but whatever comes out of a man's mouth comes from the heart and that pollutes a man, like murders, thefts, sexual vices, adulteries, lying, and slandering.

Jesus healed a woman's daughter who was possessed by demons because she showed faith. He then continued along the Sea of Galilee, healing people who all praised God. Jesus then fed a huge crowd with just seven loaves and some fish. There were at least 4000 people.

Jesus then sailed to the Magadan region. He blasted the Pharisees again for being hypocrites when they asked Him to show them a sign from Heaven. Jesus told His disciples to beware of the teachings of the Sadducees and Pharisees.

Jesus went to the district of Caesarea Philippi and asked His disciples who they thought He (the Son of Man) was. They said that He was the Christ, the Messiah, whom the Jews were expecting, and they reaffirmed their faith in Him. It was Peter who spoke up for the rest of the disciples, and Jesus said that His church would be composed of people with faith like Peter's. Jesus confirmed that He was the Son of God and told the disciples not to tell this to anyone. He explained that He had to go to Jerusalem and would suffer before being killed and raised on the third day. Anyone who wanted to walk after Him should pick up his cross and follow Him. He who wanted to save his life would lose it, but whoever lost his life for Him would find it. What advantage was it to a man to gain the whole world and lose his soul?

Jesus took Peter, James, and John to a high mountain where a bright cloud overshadowed them, and a voice from Heaven said, *"This is My Beloved Son in whom I am well pleased."* The disciples fell on their faces in fear, but Jesus reassured them and told them not to tell anyone what they had seen. They came down from the mountain, and Jesus cured the epileptic son of a man in the crowd. The disciples had not been able to cure him because, as Jesus pointed out, *"they had too little faith."*

In Galilee, Jesus told the disciples that He would be betrayed, killed, and would rise again on the third day. He then told them to go fishing and open the mouth of the first fish that they caught and they would find a coin, which should be used to pay the tax collectors. Jesus explained to the disciples that whoever humbles himself like a child will enter the Kingdom of Heaven. If your foot is lame, cut it off because it is better to enter life crippled or maimed than to be healthy and thrown in to an eternal fire. If your eye hinders you, pluck it out. If a man has a hundred sheep and one gets lost, he will leave the other ninety-nine and go and look for the lost one which, when found, would make him happier than the ninety-nine that did not stray. It is the same with God, who is not happy when any of His children stray. God is always there for those who pray and act in His Name. One should always forgive a brother's debts. Jesus concluded the lesson with the story of the master who forgave a slave owing him money. The slave, on being freed, attacked another slave for his debts. The angry master handed him over to the scourgers until he paid up.

Jesus left Galilee and went across the Jordan to Judean territory, healing the large crowds that followed. The Pharisees approached Him to test Him about divorce, and Jesus said that whoever divorced his wife for any reason, except for unfaithfulness, and married another commits adultery.

Jesus then blessed the children in the crowd. A young man asked how he could enter the Kingdom of Heaven, and Jesus told him to obey the Commandments, give everything away to the needy, and follow Him. The man went away disappointed because he had a lot of property. Jesus said that it would be difficult for a rich person to enter the Kingdom of Heaven. The first will be last and the last will be first said Jesus, after relating the story of an estate owner who paid those who came to work for him first, the same as those who came to work for him last.

Jesus then told the disciples again how He would be betrayed, handed over, sentenced to death, mocked, scourged, and crucified, only to rise again on the third day. When asked by their mother whether James and John could sit on either side of Jesus in Heaven, He replied that it was God's decision, but one must first serve and humble himself before one could be great. Jesus then healed two blind men on his way out of Jericho.

When Jesus reached Bethphage at the Mount of Olives, He sent two disciples to get him a donkey. He rode on it into Jerusalem followed by a crowd singing praises, "*Hosanna to the Son of David*," "*Hosanna in the Highest*." Jesus then entered the Temple and got angry at the traders there and overturned all their tables, saying that His house was for prayer and not a robber's den.

Jesus continued healing the blind and the lame. The Pharisees were annoyed at His popularity. Jesus left there and went to Bethany to spend the night, returning the next morning to Jerusalem. He destroyed a fig tree by just telling it to wither and then told the disciples that anything was possible if one had faith.

The chief priests and the elders asked Him who had given Him the authority to do what He was doing. Jesus refused to answer them because they did not answer His question of where they thought John the Baptist came from.

Jesus told them the parable of the man with two sons whom he told to go and work in his vineyard. One at first refused but felt sorry and later went, while the other said he would go but didn't. It was therefore the first son who had done his father's will. Tax gatherers and prostitutes would enter the Kingdom of Heaven before them (the priests) because they believed in the teaching of John the Baptist.

Jesus told another parable about the estate agent who leased out his vineyard to tenants who ended up killing his servants and son when they were sent to collect the rent. The estate agent would obviously kill the tenants and lease the vineyard to others. Jesus said that the stone, which the builders rejected, had become the chief cornerstone. In the same way, the Kingdom of God will be taken from them and given to a people who produces its fruits.

When the chief priests and the Pharisees heard His parables, they wanted to arrest Him but were afraid of the crowds who considered Him a prophet.

Jesus told another parable of the king who sent his slaves out to bring his invited guests to a wedding banquet for his son. The guests refused to come and killed his slaves, so the king attacked them with his troops and destroyed all of them. He then told his slaves to go and invite anyone they could find. One man, who was caught without his wedding robe, was tied up and thrown out into the dark. Jesus then said that in the Kingdom of Heaven, many are called, but few are chosen.

The Pharisees then tried to trick Jesus by asking Him whether it was right to pay taxes to Caesar. Jesus saw through their malice and called them hypocrites. He told them to pay to Caesar what was due to Caesar and to God what was due to God. The Pharisees marvelled at His wisdom and left Him.

The Sadducees, who don't believe in resurrection, asked Jesus that if a woman had several husbands on earth as a result of each husband dying and her being passed on to his brother, whose wife would she be at the resurrection? (In those days it was customary for a man to marry his brother's widow if she was childless when he died.) Jesus said that God is the God of Abraham, Isaac, and Jacob. He is the God of the living and not the dead. The crowds were amazed at His teachings.

The Sadducees and the Pharisees got together to test Him by asking Him what was the greatest commandment in the Law, and Jesus replied, *"You must love the Lord your God, with all your heart, soul and mind,"* and the second great commandment is, *"You must love your neighbour as yourself."* Jesus asked them who they thought Christ was the Son of, and they replied, *"David."* Then Jesus asked how come David in the Spirit calls Him Lord, saying, *"The Lord said to my Lord, sit at My right hand until I put Your enemies under Your feet"* (Psalm 110). If David had called Him *"Lord,"* then how could He be his son? No one could answer Him, and from that day on, no one tried to test Him with any more questions.

In front of the crowd, Jesus then admonished the scribes, priests, Pharisees, and Sadducees, branding them hypocrites, extortionists, fools, blind teachers, and cheats who shut the Kingdom of Heaven in people's faces preventing themselves and others from getting in. How would they escape their sentence to hell? Jesus then left the Temple, telling His disciples that the Temple would soon be destroyed.

When they were sitting on the Mount of Olives, Jesus told them that there would be wars, rumours of wars, nations and kingdoms rising against each other, earthquakes, and they would be handed over, persecuted, hated by all nations, and killed because of Him. But he who endured to the end would be saved when the world is finally destroyed. False prophets and false messiahs will come showing great wonders to mislead, but they should not believe them. The sun will go dark, so will the moon. The stars will fall out of the sky and the forces of Heaven will be shaken. Then the sign of the Son of Man will be shown in the sky, and all the tribes of earth will mourn. They will see the Son of Man with His angels coming on the clouds of Heaven with great power and glory. Then the end will come, but no one knows exactly when, except God. It will catch everybody unawares for there will be no advance warning, and just as in the days of Noah, life will proceed as normal, then everything will be destroyed.

Jesus told the story of the ten bridesmaids who bought lamps for a wedding. Five took extra oil, and five did not. The five who ran out of oil, had to go out and buy more, and while they were away, the bridegroom came and took the five who stayed and locked out the other five when they returned. When they begged to be let in, the bridegroom told them to go away as he did not know them. The same would happen when the Son of Man comes.

Jesus told the story of the master who on going away, summoned his slaves and gave one of them five talents, another two talents, and the third, one talent. When he returned, two of his slaves had doubled their money and he congratulated them, but the one who had received one talent had hid the money in the ground, accusing his master of being a miser. He was thrown out onto the streets.

The good will be separated from the bad when the Son of Man comes, and everyone will be judged by what good or bad they did on earth. Those who did bad would go into eternal punishment and those who did good, into eternal life. Jesus then told His disciples that the Passover would be celebrated after two days, and He would be handed over and crucified.

Led by Caiaphas, the chief priests plotted to arrest Jesus and kill Him, but decided to wait until after the Feast of the Passover. Jesus reprimanded His disciples for getting annoyed with a woman who poured precious perfume on His head, saying that she was preparing Him for His burial and what she had done would be remembered wherever the gospel was preached.

Judas went to the priests and accepted the bribe of thirty pieces of silver to betray Jesus.

That evening, Jesus sat with His disciples for the last supper, eating the Passover. He told them that one of them would betray Him and it would be better for that person if he had not been born. Judas then asked if Jesus thought it was him. Jesus replied, *"You have said it."* Jesus took bread, gave thanks, and broke it for His disciples to eat, saying it was His Body. He then took some wine, gave thanks, and gave them to drink, saying it was His Blood, poured out for the forgiveness of sins.

Later, they all went up to the Mount of Olives where Jesus told them that they would all desert Him, but after He was raised up from the dead, He would precede them to Galilee. When Peter denied he would ever desert him, Jesus said that he would deny Him three times before the cock crowed.

Jesus then went with them to Gethsemane and told them to wait for Him while He went to pray, taking only Peter, James, and John with Him. He felt depressed and fell on His face to pray to God. He returned and admonished them for sleeping. He left them twice more to pray, and each time he returned, they were sleeping. He told them that His hour had come because He could see His betrayer.

Judas came with the chief priests and a large mob that arrested Jesus after he had kissed Him. One of the disciples cut off the ear of one of the slaves arresting Jesus, who blasted him to put his sword away, saying that all this was supposed to happen. All the disciples ran away from Him.

He was taken to Caiaphas where He was questioned, but they could find nothing wrong with Him despite many false witnesses. Only when they asked him if He was the Son of God and He said that they would shortly see Him seated on the right hand of God, did they feel they had enough blasphemous evidence to kill Him.

They beat Him up and spat on Him. Peter had secretly followed them when they took Jesus away and sat outside in the courtyard. On being recognized thrice by slave girls as one of Jesus' followers, he thrice denied it. A rooster immediately crowed, and Peter remembered what Jesus had earlier said and started crying bitterly.

The chief priests and the elders held a meeting at dawn and agreed to execute Jesus. They tied Him up and handed Him over to Pilate the governor. When Judas saw this, he felt remorse and returned the thirty pieces of silver to the chief priests who dismissed him. He flung the money down in the Temple, ran off, and hanged himself. They picked up the money, which they used to buy the *"Potter's Field"* as a cemetery for strangers, exactly what Jeremiah had earlier prophesied (Jeremiah 19). The field was from then on called *"The Field of Blood."*

Pilate asked Jesus if He was the King of the Jews and whether He understood the accusations levelled against Him. On both occasions Jesus remained silent. In those days, it was customary for the governor to release at the feast one prisoner selected by the populace. So Pilate, on realising that Jesus was innocent and was only brought to him through envy, asked whether he should release Barabbas, the most notorious criminal, or Jesus. The crowd shouted for Barabbas.

Pilate's wife quietly told him that he should leave Jesus because of a disturbing dream that she had had.

Pilate publicly washed his hands in front of the crowd, claiming his innocence. The crowd shouted, *"Crucify Him and let His Blood be on us and our children!"* Pilate released Barabbas but flogged Jesus and handed Him over to be crucified.

The people put a purple robe on Him, a crown of thorns on His head, and a reed in His hand before ridiculing Him with taunts of *"Long live the King of the Jews!"* and beating and spitting on Him. They took Him away to be crucified. On the way, they forced a Cyrenian called Simon to carry His cross for Him. At Golgotha (Place of the Skull), they gave Him wine mixed with gall (a bitter painkilling drug) to drink, but after tasting it, Jesus refused to drink it as He wanted to be fully conscious up to the end.

After crucifying Him, they drew lots and shared His clothes amongst themselves. They put a sign above Him on the cross, saying *"INRI" (IESUS NAZARENUS REX IU-DAEORUM)* meaning Jesus of Nazareth, King of the Jews. Two robbers were also crucified alongside Him.

The crowds taunted Him saying that if He was the Son of God, He should come down from the cross and God should save Him. There was darkness for three hours everywhere, and Jesus, on dying, shouted, *"Eli Eli, Lama Sabachthani"* (My God My God, why have You forsaken Me). Some bystanders soaked a sponge in vinegar and offered it to Him to drink. After crying out once more, He died.

The veil of the Temple was torn in two from top to bottom, the earth shook, tombs were opened, and many bodies of buried saints were raised. The soldiers watching Jesus were afraid on seeing the earthquake and agreed that Jesus really was the Son of God. Mary Magdalene and Mary, the mother of the Zebedee brothers, James and John, both saw what had happened.

Joseph of Arimathea went to Pilate and requested the Body of Jesus, which he wrapped in clean clothes and put into his own new tomb. The priests, however, requested soldiers from Pilate to guard the tomb in case the body was stolen. On the third day, an angel rolled away the stone and sat on it, followed by an earthquake. The soldiers collapsed in fear.

The two Marys, who had come to look at the tomb, were told by the angel that Jesus had risen and that they should go and tell the disciples that He would meet them in Galilee.

The soldiers were given bribe money by the priests to say that the disciples had come and stolen the body.

The eleven disciples went to the mountain and saw Jesus. They bowed down and worshipped Him. He said that God had given Him all the authority on earth and in Heaven and that they should go out and baptise the whole world in the Name of the Father, the Son and the Holy Spirit, and that they should remember that He would always be with them to the end of the world.

THE GOSPEL ACCORDING
TO MARK

John the Baptist was preaching and baptising people in the river Jordan when he told the people of Jerusalem that he was baptising them with water but someone greater than he would come and baptise them with the Holy Spirit.

Jesus came one day and was baptised by John. As soon as He came out of the water, the heavens parted, and the Spirit came down upon Him followed by a voice from Heaven, which said, *"You are My Son, My Beloved in whom I am well pleased."*

The Spirit drove Jesus to the desert where He spent forty days being tempted by Satan. He was with the wild beasts, and the angels waited on Him.

After John had been arrested, Jesus went to Galilee, preaching God's Word and telling the people to repent. Along the Sea of Galilee, He saw Simon and his brother Andrew throwing a net into the sea, and He told them to follow Him and He would make them fishers of men. They left their nets and followed Him. James and John, sons of Zebedee, also left their father in a boat and followed Him.

They went to Capernaum and went into a synagogue and taught. A man with an unclean spirit started shouting that Jesus was the Holy One of God. Jesus said, *"Silence, get out of him,"* and the man threw a spasm, cried out loud, and the spirit came out of him. The people were so amazed, His fame spread throughout Galilee. Jesus then cured Simon and Andrew's mother of fever at their house. Jesus cured all the sick and demoniacs until the whole city was standing outside the door.

The next morning before dawn, He went out to a lonely spot to pray and later went to the adjoining towns to preach in their synagogues and cast out the demons. He cured a leper and warned him not to tell anyone but he should rather go and offer what Moses had prescribed for his purification, as a testimony to the people. But he went and told everybody, who all came to Jesus.

Jesus returned to Capernaum, and people congregated at His home. A paralytic was lowered through the roof to Him, and Jesus cured him. The people were so amazed they glorified God. The scribes were wondering who this Man was who could forgive sins and heal the crippled, thinking that it was blasphemous.

Jesus continued healing and teaching. He met Levi, the son of Alphaeus, sitting at the tax office, and He told him to follow Him. When the people wondered what He was doing talking to sinners and tax collectors, Jesus replied that it was not the healthy but the sick that needed a physician. He did not come to call the righteous, but the sinners.

One day, the Pharisees were observing a fast, which the disciples were not, so they came and asked Jesus why. Jesus replied that the wedding guests cannot fast when the bridegroom is around, but the day will come when the bridegroom will be taken from them and that will be their time to fast. No one sews a patch of unshrunken cloth on an old coat, and no one pours new wine into old wine skins.

When the disciples started picking heads of wheat in a wheat field, the Pharisees complained that this was not done on a Sabbath day. Jesus explained that the Sabbath was made for man's sake and not man for the Sabbath, so the Son of Man is also Lord of the Sabbath. When Jesus cured a man with a withered hand on the Sabbath, the Pharisees were annoyed, and they left to plot against Him with the Herodians.

Jesus then went with His disciples to the beach, followed by many people. He healed so many that they all came close just to touch Him. He then went up the hill with His twelve disciples, Simon Peter, James, and John the sons of Zebedee (whom He called Boanerges, meaning sons of thunder), Andrew and Philip, Bartholomew and Matthew, Thomas and James (the son of Alphaeus), Thaddeus, Simon of Cana, and Judas Iscariot.

Some scribes accused Him of using Satan to expel Satan. Jesus rejected this and explained that in order to rob a strong man's house, one first had to subdue the strong man. All sins were pardonable except the ones against the Holy Spirit. When told that His mother and His brothers were looking for Him, Jesus said that anyone who obeyed God's will was His brother, sister, and mother.

Jesus continued teaching by the seaside and always spoke in parables. He started with the parable of the sower saying that if they didn't understand that, how would they understand any of them? He then proceeded to explain how it was connected to the Kingdom of God. The Kingdom of God is like when a man scatters seed in the soil, then sleeps at night and rises by day while the seed sprouts and springs up. He will never know how. It is like the mustard seed, smaller than any seed, yet when it sprouts it grows to be larger than any plant, producing such large branches that the birds can rest under its shelter.

They left the crowd and went into the boat followed by other boats. Jesus reprimanded the disciples for being afraid of the storm and not having any faith. They were amazed when He calmed the waves, saying, *"Who is this man? For even the wind and the sea obey Him!"*

They arrived at Gerasenes where Jesus cured a madman of a legion of evil spirits and putting them into a herd of two thousand pigs that ran down a precipice into a lake and drowned. The news spread like wildfire, and people rushed to the scene to see what had happened. The madman was told to go home and tell everyone what God had done for him.

A synagogue director called Jairus came to beg Jesus to cure his daughter who had died. Jesus went to the house and told her family that she was asleep and not dead. He told her to get up, and she got up. Jesus told them to give her some food and not to tell anyone what had happened. On the way there, a woman was cured of her haemorrhages by touching Jesus' robe. Jesus told her to go in peace for her faith had healed her.

Jesus began to teach in a synagogue in His hometown on the Sabbath, and people were amazed at His wisdom. Some people took offense at His knowledge, and Jesus replied that a prophet is always without honour in his own country. Jesus continued healing the sick and sent out His disciples to teach and heal on His behalf, which they did.

When Herod heard about Jesus, he thought He was John the Baptist, whom he had beheaded, back from the dead. John had been killed for not agreeing for Herod to marry Heroidas, the wife of his brother Philip. Heroidas' daughter was promised anything she liked by Herod for dancing on his birthday, and she asked for John the Baptist's head.

When Jesus heard this, He and His disciples left by boat to preach elsewhere and fed a huge crowd of five thousand with five loaves and two fish. The disciples left the people by boat and left Jesus with them. Later, they saw Jesus walking on the waves towards them during a storm. They were afraid, and Jesus told them to take courage and not be afraid, then he calmed the waves.

They landed at Gennesaret, and the crowd came to Him with all their sick. When asked by the Pharisees why the disciples ate without washing their hands, Jesus reprimanded them for ignoring God to suit themselves and said that it was what came out of a man that made a person unclean and not what went into his mouth. Things like murder, theft, unchastity, adultery, greed, wickedness, deceit, licentiousness, vicious envy, blasphemy, pride, and foolishness all come from the heart and defile a man. Jesus then cured the demons out of a woman's daughter.

Returning from Tyre, He passed through Sidon on the Sea of Galilee to the Decapolis region where He cured a deaf and dumb man by simply looking towards Heaven and saying, "*Ephphatha*" (meaning "be opened"). The more He told them not to tell anyone, the more His fame spread. Jesus felt sorry for a crowd that had followed Him for three days without food, so with just seven loaves and some fish, He was able to feed about four thousand people.

He left them and went to Dalmanutha with His disciples. When the Pharisees asked Him for a sign from Heaven, Jesus refused and left them. He reprimanded His disciples for complaining about having no food as if they had not seen Him feed the four thousand people.

Jesus then healed a blind man at Bethsaida. He asked His disciples who the people thought He was, and they replied, "John the Baptist" but they believed He was the Christ. Jesus told them not to tell anyone. He told them He would suffer, be rejected by the chief priests and scribes, and be executed. He would, however, rise again after three days. If anyone wanted to go with Him, that person should pick up his cross and follow Him. Whoever wishes to save his life will lose it, and whoever loses his life on account of Him and the Gospel will save it. What profit is there to a man who gains the whole world only to lose his soul?

Six days later, Jesus took Peter, James, and John to the top of a mountain where Jesus' robes became a brilliant white, and Elijah appeared with Moses and talked to Jesus. A cloud then appeared, and a voice came from it saying, "*This is My Son, the Beloved, listen to Him.*" Suddenly, Jesus was alone again. He told them not to tell anyone what they had seen.

When they came down from the mountain, a crowd had gathered there, and Jesus cured an epileptic boy. Jesus told His disciples that the kind of evil spirit in the boy could be expelled only through prayer.

They passed through Galilee, and Jesus again told His disciples that He would be killed and rise again three days later. Jesus was teaching His disciples that whoever receives a child in His Name, receives Him. The first shall be last, and the last shall be first. Anyone who wants to be first must first of all be a servant, and anyone who does something good in His Name will always be rewarded. If your foot causes you to sin, cut it off because it is better to be crippled or maimed in life than to be all right and go to hell.

Jesus then went to the Judean region followed by crowds, and He taught on divorce. It was wrong to divorce because no man should divide what God has joined. Whoever divorces and marries another commits adultery. He told them always to let children come to Him because whoever fails to receive the Kingdom of Heaven like a child will never enter it.

A man came to Him and asked Him how he could have eternal life, and Jesus told him to obey the Commandments, give away all his property to the poor, and follow Him. He went away sad because he was a wealthy man. Jesus said it was easier for a camel to pass through the eye of a needle than for a rich man to enter the Kingdom of God.

Jesus reiterated that He was going to be delivered to the chief priests, executed, and would rise again after the third day. When the disciples asked Jesus to sit on His right side in Heaven, He told them that only God could decide that but He would never deny them anything that He had.

They then came to Jericho where Jesus cured Bartimaeus, a blind beggar who called on Him to help him.

They were near Jerusalem when Jesus sent two of His disciples to get a colt that no one had ever ridden. They found one, and Jesus sat on it and rode into Jerusalem followed by a crowd shouting, "*Hosanna in the Highest.*"

He went into the Temple and observed what was going on. He then knocked over all the tables and chairs belonging to the moneychangers and sellers, saying that it was wrong to trade in the Temple. The chief priests looked for a way to destroy Him.

He then told a fig tree not to grow anymore, and it immediately withered. Jesus did this in order to show them that anything was possible with faith.

When the priests asked Him by whose authority He was preaching and healing, Jesus asked them by whose authority was John the Baptist baptising people? When they could not answer, Jesus then told them the parable of the man and his vineyard that he leased out to some tenants who kept on killing anyone he sent to them to collect the rent, including his own son. Jesus said it meant that the owner would come and put the tenants to death and lease the vineyard to others. The stone that the others rejected had become the head of the corner. The Pharisees, looking for ways to arrest Him, asked Him if it was right to pay tax to Caesar, so Jesus asked whose face was on the coins and when they replied, "*Caesar*," He said they should pay to Caesar what belongs to Caesar and to God what belongs to God.

The Sadducees who don't believe in resurrection tried to trap Jesus by asking about the resurrection of the husband of a woman who in this life was married seven times. The woman was married to a man and had no child when he died. The woman was passed on seven times to brothers of the first husband, and none of them produced a child. (In those days a brother was obliged to take his widowed sister-in-law so that she would have a child to support her when she grew old.) Jesus said that their question revealed ignorance about the afterlife. Abraham must still be alive if God can call himself the God of Abraham for He is a God of the living and not the dead.

When asked which of the commandments was the main Commandment, Jesus said, "*You should love the Lord your God with your whole heart, soul, mind and strength. The next is you should love your neighbour as yourself. That is more important than all the burnt offerings.*" After that no one tried to question Jesus any more. Jesus concluded by saying that those who enjoy life at the expense of others, like the scribes, would receive harsher sentences.

A woman came and put two mites (about a penny) into a collection box, and Jesus said that what she had done was greater than all the rich men's offerings because they put of their surplus whilst she put in all that she had.

As Jesus left the Temple, He said that it would soon be destroyed, and no stone would be left on another. He told His disciples that one day the world would be destroyed by earthquake, famine, revolts, and wars. Many would come claiming to be Him but when they hear rumours about wars or His Coming, they should not be alarmed because it must be so. They will be flogged and appear before councils, governors, and kings because of Him.

First, the Gospel must be preached to all nations. When they were arrested, they should just speak what comes into their mouths because it would not be they but the Holy Spirit speaking. Families would be torn against one another, and they would be hated by everyone because of Him; but whoever perseveres to the end would be saved.

False prophets and fake Christs would come from time to time and perform wonders in order to lead people astray, but they should be on their guard and not be deceived. The end will come when the sun and the moon will be darkened. The stars will fall from the sky and they will see the Son of Man coming in the clouds with great power and glory and His angels will collect the chosen few. When they see these signs, they will know that the end is near. No one knows the exact time except God. So they should watch because no one knows when it will happen.

The disciples reprimanded a woman who poured expensive perfume on Jesus' head, but He said that she had done well in preparing His Body for burial. This was in Bethany at the house of Simon the leper. By that time Judas Iscariot had gone to the chief priests, and they promised him money to betray Jesus.

Jesus sat with His disciples eating the Passover supper when He said that one of them would betray Him, and it would be better for him if he had not been born. As the meal proceeded, Jesus took bread, broke it, and gave thanks saying it was His Body. He did the same with the wine, which they drank. He said it was His Blood of the Covenant. He would not drink any more until He was in God's Kingdom. They sang a hymn and went out to the Mount of Olives where Jesus told them that they would all turn against Him. When Peter denied this, Jesus told him that he would deny Him three times before the cock crowed.

They went to Gethsemane, and the disciples waited for Jesus while He went further on with Peter, James, and John to pray. He told them to wait for Him while He prayed. He returned three times, each time to find them sleeping and told them that their spirit was willing but their flesh was weak.

He was still talking when Judas came with a great mob holding swords and clubs. Judas kissed Jesus, and the mob grabbed Him and arrested Him. One of the disciples cut off the ear of one of the slaves. Jesus asked them why they did not arrest Him before when He was preaching in the Temple and that all this was happening in order to fulfil the Scriptures. The disciples all ran away and left Him.

They took Him to the high priest who questioned Him, but there was not sufficient evidence to convict Him, despite the false witnesses they had lined up. Jesus kept quiet and refused to answer them. They asked Him if He was Christ, the Son of God, and Jesus replied in the affirmative, saying that they would soon see Him seated at the right hand of God. They accused Him of blasphemy, spat on Him, beat Him, and blindfolded Him.

Three servant girls, who saw Peter hanging around the courtyard outside, asked him if he was the one with Jesus. On each occasion, Peter denied it, and after the final time, the cock crowed. He then remembered what Jesus had said and started crying loudly.

The next morning, Jesus was sent by the chief priests to Pontius Pilate who asked Him if He was the King of the Jews. Jesus did not answer, making Pilate wonder whether the charges against Him were true.

At the feast, it was customary for him to release a prisoner to the crowd, and Pilate asked whether he should release Jesus because he knew that it was out of envy that they had brought Jesus to him. Instead, the crowd shouted for him to release Barabbas, the most notorious murderer and criminal. When Pilate asked what should be done to Jesus, they shouted, *"Crucify Him!"* The crowd were so vociferous that Pilate did not want to annoy them and released Barabbas to them. He had Jesus flogged and handed over.

The crowd dressed Him in purple and put a crown of thorns on His head. They beat Him, spat on Him, and taunted Him with *"Long live the King of the Jews."* They forced a passerby called Simon to carry His cross. Jesus refused the wine, flavoured with myrrh, which they offered Him.

He was then taken to Golgotha (Place of the Skull) and was crucified. They cast lots to divide His clothes. On top of the cross was written, *"The King of the Jews."* Two robbers were also crucified either side of Him. The people taunted Him saying that He had saved others but could not save Himself. Even the robbers next to Him teased Him.

There was darkness everywhere between midday and three o'clock, and at three o'clock, Jesus said with a loud voice, *"Eli, Eli, Lama Sabachtani,"* meaning, *"My God, My God, why have You forsaken Me?"* One person in the crowd soaked some vinegar in a sponge, fixed it on to a stick, and gave Him a drink, saying that He was shouting for Elijah, and they wanted to see if Elijah would bring Him down. Jesus uttered a strong cry and died. The Temple veil was torn in two from top to bottom. The centurion guarding Him said, *"Truly this Man was God's Son."*

Mary Magdalene, Mary the mother of Jesus, and Salome, a woman who had been following Him and helping Him in Galilee, also saw Him die.

Joseph of Arimathea boldly asked Pilate for Jesus' body. When it was confirmed that He was dead, Pilate allowed him to take the body. He wrapped Jesus in a linen sheet, laid Him in a tomb carved of rock, and rolled a stone against the opening.

The next day, Mary Magdalene, Mary the mother of James, and Salome took some spices to the body but found that the stone had been rolled away. They went into the tomb and saw a man sitting there dressed in white who told them that Jesus had risen.

Jesus first appeared to Mary Magdalene from whom He had expelled seven demons. She went and told her friends, who did not believe her. Jesus also appeared to two of the women and later to the disciples and chided them for their disbelief and hardheartedness because they did not believe He had risen. Jesus told them to go out into the world and preach the Gospel to everybody. He who believes will be baptised and saved, and he who does not believe will be condemned. His Name will heal, cure, and expel demons. It will perform miracles for those who believe.

After that, Jesus went up to Heaven and sat on the right Hand of God. The disciples went out and preached everywhere because God was working with them and confirming the Message by the signs that followed.

THE GOSPEL ACCORDING TO LUKE

In the days of Herod king of Judea, Zechariah a priest had
a vision of the angel Gabriel while he was in the Temple
burning incense. He had no children, so Gabriel told him
that his wife Elizabeth, although old in years, would bear a
child and he was to be called John. He would grow up to be
great, God fearing, and filled with the Holy Spirit. He would
turn many people towards God. Gabriel told him that he
would be struck dumb until the day when these things took
place. When Zechariah came out of the Temple, he could not
speak, and the people knew he had seen a vision.

Elizabeth conceived and hid herself for five months. In the
sixth month of Elizabeth's pregnancy, Gabriel appeared to
her cousin, a virgin called Mary who was engaged to Joseph,
a descendant of King David, and told her that she would bear
a Son who was to be called Jesus. He would be great and
called Son of the Highest and be King over the House of
Jacob forever. When Mary asked how this was possible as
she was not yet married, the angel said that the Holy Spirit
would come on her and the boy would be a holy offspring
called the Son of God.

Mary went to see Elizabeth, and they were both filled with
the Holy Spirit. Mary stayed with her for about three months
and then went home. Elizabeth gave birth, and they called
the baby John. Zechariah was now able to speak, and his first
words were, "*His name is John.*" The child grew up and was
spiritually strengthened by God.

An order went out from Caesar Augustus for a census of
the whole world to be taken. Joseph went with his pregnant
fiancée Mary to be registered. Mary gave birth and wrapped
Jesus in swaddling clothes (bands of cloth in which newly

born babies were wrapped in) and laid Him in a manger because there was no room for them at the inn.

An angel appeared to some shepherds to give them the
good news about the birth of Christ. The shepherds were
afraid, but the angel appeased them by saying where they
would find the baby wrapped in swaddling clothes. A group
of angels appeared singing, *"Glory to God in the highest and
on earth peace among men,"* in His favour. The shepherds
went quickly to Bethlehem and saw Jesus. They told everybody what they had heard about the baby, and then they went
away, praising God for everything.

After eight days, the child was circumcised and given
the name Jesus. Mary, His mother, was purified. They then
brought Him to Jerusalem to present Him to God as was prescribed by God's Law.

There was a man called Simeon who was told by the
Holy Spirit that he would not see death until he had seen
the Christ. He went into the Temple and held Jesus in his
arms. He was so happy he thanked and praised the Lord saying what we now know as the *"Nunc Dimittis."* Simeon then
blessed Joseph and Mary saying that Jesus was destined to
cause the falling and rising of many in Israel and for a sign
that would be opposed. A prophetess called Anna also came
and blessed them, giving thanks to God, and saying good
things about Jesus concerning the redemption of Jerusalem.

They returned to Galilee, and Jesus grew up filled with
wisdom, and God's Grace was with Him.

When Jesus was twelve years old, He went with His parents to Jerusalem to celebrate the Passover feast. As they
were returning, it was discovered that Jesus was not with
them. His parents searched everywhere for Him and eventually found Him still in Jerusalem in the Temple, listening to
the elders and asking questions. All who heard Him were
astounded at His understanding and His answers. When His
mother asked Him why He had treated them in this way,
Jesus asked why they had been looking for Him as they

should have known that He was in His Father's house doing His Father's business. His parents did not understand what He was saying. Jesus grew big and wise and in favour with both God and men.

In the fifteenth year of Tiberius Caesar's reign when Pontius Pilate was governor of Judea, the Word of God came to John (Son of Zechariah) in the desert. He went to the Jordan River, preaching, baptising, and telling people to follow God's ways and repent. He said people should love one another and share everything. Soldiers should not extort money, intimidate, or inform on people, but they should be content with their pay. People wondered whether John was the Christ, but he said that someone greater than he would come and baptise them not with water, like he did, but with the Holy Spirit.

When John told Herod that it was wrong of him to marry Heroidas (his brother Philip's wife), Herod threw him into prison. Jesus was one of the people baptised by John, only at that time the Holy Spirit came down in the shape of a dove, and a voice from Heaven said, *"You are My Beloved Son; in You I am well pleased."*

Jesus was about thirty years old when He began His Ministry. He was descended from Joseph all the way through Joshua, Eliezar, Levi, Simeon, Joseph, Eliakim, David, Judah, Jacob, Isaac, Abraham, Shem, Noah, Adam, and finally to God.

Jesus went to the desert for forty days where He was tempted by the devil who promised Him all the world's kingdoms if He would worship him. Jesus said, *"It is written, you will worship the Lord your God and serve Him alone."* When Satan told Him to turn a piece of stone into bread, Jesus said, *"Man shall not live by bread alone"* and when Satan told Him to jump from the top of the Temple, Jesus replied, *"It is also written, you shall not test the Lord your God."* So Satan left Him, and Jesus returned to Galilee and taught in the synagogues.

He went to one on the Sabbath and read quotations from the book of Isaiah from a scroll. Jesus said no prophet is acceptable in his hometown. The people were resentful at His teachings and expelled Him from their city.

Jesus went to Capernaum where He cured a man possessed by evil spirits who claimed he knew that Jesus was the Holy One of God. Jesus said, *"Be still and get out of him!"* and the demon left him. The people were so amazed, His Name spread throughout the surrounding country. He cured everyone who came to Him with diseases or evil spirits.

As He was preaching by Lake Gennesaret, He noticed Simon Peter having problems catching fish, and He told him to go out deeper. Simon Peter said he had been trying all night with no success, but as soon as he did what Jesus had advised, he caught so much fish that his net started breaking. He called his partners to bring another boat, which almost sunk because they had caught so much fish. Peter fell at the feet of Jesus who told him, *"Have no fear; from now on you will be catching men."* Together with James and John, the sons of Zebedee, they left everything and followed Jesus.

Jesus cured a leper and warned him not to tell anyone but instead to go to a priest and make offerings for his purification as Moses had prescribed, as evidence to the people. Jesus became more and more famous and habitually withdrew into the desert to pray.

On one occasion when Jesus was teaching, some people who could not get close to Him carried a paralytic on a couch through the roof and put him down at Jesus' feet. Jesus cured him saying, *"Your sins are forgiven,"* because of their faith. The Pharisees were annoyed because only God had the power to forgive sins. So Jesus told the man to rise up, pick up his mat, and walk home. The people were amazed when the man started walking.

One day, Levi, a tax collector, was having a banquet at his house for Jesus, and several tax collectors were also there, so when He was asked why He mixed with sinners and tax collectors, Jesus said that healthy people did not need a physician. He did not come to call the upright to repentance, but the sinners.

When they complained that the disciples were eating, Jesus said that one could not expect people to starve in front of the bridegroom at his wedding but the time would come when the bridegroom would be gone and then they would fast. Then Jesus said no one patches an old garment with a new patch and no one pours new wine into old wine skins, and besides, no one who is used to drinking old wine wants new wine right away because he prefers the old one.

When His disciples picked the heads of grain in a grain field and ate them, the Pharisees asked Him why they were practising what was not allowed on the Sabbath, and Jesus replied that even David ate in God's house when he was hungry and that the Son of Man was Lord of the Sabbath. The Pharisees were so angry that they plotted against Jesus.

Jesus then went to the hills to pray and got twelve disciples together to work with Him. They were Simon Peter, his brother Andrew, James and John, Philip, Bartholomew, Matthew, Thomas, James (son of Alphaeus), Simon the zealot, Judas (son of James), and Judas Iscariot. Jesus healed everybody who came to hear Him preach. He explained what we now know as the *"Beatitudes"* to the people, as a way of showing them the right way to live. One should love his enemy and treat well those who hate him. Bless those who curse you and pray for those who abuse you. Anybody who suffers on earth on account of Him will be richly rewarded in Heaven.

Those who are hungry now will be full later. Those who are sad now will be happy later. Those who are poor will have the Kingdom of God. If someone strikes your cheek, give him the other one, and always give to anyone who asks, without asking for anything back. Treat others exactly as you would like them to treat you. Don't only give to those you expect something back from.

Love your enemies and be merciful because God is merciful. Do not judge or condemn, and it will not happen to you.

Pardon and you will be pardoned. Do not be a hypocrite. First remove the beam from your eye before you can see clearly to extract the splinter from your brother's eye.

No good tree bears worthless fruit. The good person expresses good from the good that is stored in his heart and the evil person expresses evil from the evil that is stored in his heart. Those who listen and do as He says are like the man who built a house with a solid foundation. Nothing can shake it or destroy it.

Jesus went to Capernaum and met a centurion who asked Him to cure his slave without even coming to his house because he was not worthy to have Him under his roof. All Jesus had to do was say the word and the slave would be healed. Jesus said that He had not found anybody with as much faith as the centurion, who returned home and found his slave healed.

Jesus went to a town called Nain where he brought a widow's only son, who had died and was on the way to being buried, back to life. Jesus' fame spread even more as people praised and glorified God. Some people came to Jesus with a message from John the Baptist asking if Jesus was indeed the Coming One. Jesus told them to tell John what they had seen-the blind were made to see, the lame could now walk, lepers had been cleansed, the deaf could hear, the dead were raised, and the poor evangelised.

Blessed is he who does not turn away from Him. Jesus told the crowd that John the Baptist was great but even the least person in the Kingdom of Heaven was greater than he. Everybody then acknowledged God as just, except the Pharisees and the teachers who had always refused baptism under John.

Jesus went for dinner at the house of a Pharisee where a prostitute and sinner washed His feet with her tears, cleaned them with her hair, and put perfume on them. The Pharisee wondered why Jesus allowed this from a sinner.

Jesus told them the parable of a man who cancelled the debts of two men, one with a big debt and the other with a small debt. Jesus asked which one would love the man more, and the Pharisee said the one with the bigger debt. Jesus said he was correct. He had come to his house, and he had not even offered Him water to wash His feet nor given Him oil for His hair, yet this woman had done the best with what she had for Him. Jesus then told the woman that her sins were forgiven, and she should go because her faith had saved her. The people at the dinner began to wonder who Jesus thought He was by forgiving sins.

Jesus travelled through many towns, and villages preaching the good news of God followed by His disciples and several women who had been cured of evil spirits, including Mary Magdalene from whom several demons had been expelled.

In front of a great crowd, Jesus told them the parable of the sower. A sower sowed some seeds. Some fell on the path and was walked on, and the birds ate them. Others fell on bedrock and sprouted, but withered because they lacked moisture. Others fell on thorns, grew with them, but were choked, and the rest fell on good soil, grew up, and yielded a hundredfold.

Asked for explanation Jesus said, the seed was the Word of God. The ones that fell on the path are the people who hear and the devil comes and carries away the Word from their hearts so that they do not believe and are not saved. Those on the bedrock are people who hear the Word and welcome it gladly but have no root, so they believe for a while but in time of trial they fall away. The ones that fell on thorns are the people who listen but as they go on, the Word is choked by worries, wealth, and pleasures of life so that they never mature. But the seed in the good soil are those who listen to the Word, retain it in a good and well-disposed heart, and steadily bear fruit.

Nothing is hidden that will not be disclosed. Look out how you listen, for whoever has will receive more, and the one who has nothing, what he fancies he possesses will be taken away from him. Jesus' mother and brothers came to

Him but could not get close because of the crowd. When told this, Jesus replied that anyone who hears and practises the Word of God is His mother and His brother.

One day, Jesus and His disciples were on a boat that went into a storm. They panicked and told Jesus they were sinking. Jesus calmed the waves and rebuked them for their lack of faith. They were awed and amazed asking themselves, *"Who is He anyway, to give orders to the winds and water and they obey Him?"*

They landed at the Gerasenes, a country opposite Galilee, and He cured a man possessed by demons called Legion. The people who had known the madman a long time were surprised to see him sane and were afraid, so they asked Jesus to leave. Jesus got back into the boat and told the madman to go and tell everyone what God had done for him.

Jesus returned to Galilee and was met by a huge crowd. One of them, Jairus, a ruler of the synagogue, begged Jesus to cure his daughter who was dying. On the way to the man's house, a woman who had haemorrhage touched His clothes, and she was cured. Jesus noticed, and the woman fell on her knees and confessed. Jesus said, *"Daughter, cheer up. Your faith has healed you; go in peace."*

On reaching Jairus' house, Jesus went in with Peter, James, and John and was told the girl was already dead. Jesus told her to get up, and her spirit returned. He told them to give her some food and not tell anyone what had happened.

Jesus then gave His disciples the power to heal and exorcise evil spirits then sent them out to preach the Kingdom of God and to heal the sick. If they were not welcome at some places, Jesus told them to shake the dust from their feet as a testimony against them and leave.

When Herod heard about what Jesus had been doing, he was worried because he had beheaded John the Baptist, and people were saying that he had come back to life.

The disciples returned to report everything they had done, and Jesus took them to a town called Bethsaida, but the crowds followed them, and He continued to talk to them and heal them. When the disciples told Jesus the crowd had no food, Jesus turned five loaves and two fish into enough food to feed five thousand people with twelve baskets full of leftovers.

When Jesus was praying by Himself, the disciples came to Him, and He told them that it was true He was the Christ and He would suffer many things, be rejected by the chief priests and scribes, and be executed, but on the third day, He would rise from the dead. Anyone who wants to come after Him must deny himself, pick up a cross, and follow Him. Whoever wants to save his life will lose it, but whoever loses his life because of Him will save it. What benefit is there for a person who gains the whole world only to lose or forfeit himself? Whoever is ashamed of Him and His teachings will find that the Son of Man will be ashamed of him when He comes in His own glory, and some will not taste death until they see the Kingdom of God.

Jesus took Peter, James, and John to a mountain where He prayed. His clothes turned to dazzling white as Moses and Elijah appeared and talked to Him about His departure, which He was to accomplish at Jerusalem. A cloud covered them, and the disciples heard a voice saying, *"This is My Son, My Chosen One. Listen to Him."* The cloud disappeared, and Jesus was alone.

The next day, they came down from the mountain where Jesus cured an epileptic boy who was having convulsions. The people were all amazed, and Jesus said to His disciples that He would be delivered into human hands; but they did not understand Him. Jesus then picked up a child and told the crowd that whoever receives a child in His Name receives Him, and He who sent Him. When told that someone was expelling demons in His Name, Jesus said that anyone who was not against Him was for Him.

When one village refused to accept Jesus, the disciples wanted to send fire from Heaven to destroy them, but Jesus said that He did not come to destroy lives but to save them. *"Let the dead bury their own dead. Anyone who puts his*

*hand to the plough and looks back is not fit for the Kingdom
of God.*"
Jesus then commissioned seventy others to go to different
towns, preaching and healing. He told them only to go to
the houses in which they were welcome. They returned with
good news for Jesus, who told them that they should not be
happy that they were able to exorcise evil spirits, but they
should be happy because their names had been registered in
Heaven. Everything has been handed to Him by His Father,
and no one knows who the Father is except the Son and vice
versa. They should be happy that they were experiencing
Him and His miracles because many prophets and kings in
the past had longed to see what they were seeing but could
not.

A teacher asked Him what he should do to inherit eternal
life, and Jesus asked him what was written in the Law. The
man replied that one should love the Lord his God with all
his heart, soul, strength, and mind and his neighbour as himself. Jesus told him to do that and he would live.

When the teacher asked Him who his neighbour was,
Jesus told him the parable of the good Samaritan who helped
a man he did not know, who had been attacked by robbers
and left dying on the road. A priest and a Levite had both
walked past him and had ignored him, but the Samaritan felt
sorry for him, bandaged his wounds, put him on his own
donkey, and put him in an inn, even paying the innkeeper to
look after him. Jesus told the teacher to go and do the same.

Jesus went to the home of two sisters, Mary and Martha.
When Martha complained that Mary was busy listening to
Him and had left all the housework for her to do, Jesus said
that Mary had done the right thing and that will not be taken
from her.

The disciples one day saw Jesus praying and asked Him to
teach them how to pray. Jesus taught them the *Lord's Prayer*
and told them, "*Ask and it shall be given, seek and you shall
find, knock and it will be opened to you.*" Nobody would refuse his child anything so how much more would God give

the Holy Spirit to those who ask Him. Jesus cured a dumb man and told the crowd that He expels demons not through Beelzebul or Satan but rather through God. He who is not with Him is against Him.

A woman praised Jesus by saying, *"Blessed is the womb that bore You and the breasts on which You nursed."*

Jesus replied, *"More blessed are those who hear and keep the Word of God."*

Jesus said that the generation they were in was an evil generation that was looking for a sign and only that of Jonah would be given to it. As Jonah was the sign of the Ninevites (the inhabitants of Nineveh, the former capital of the Assyrian empire founded by Nimrod a great-grandson of Noah), so would He be the sign for this generation. Something greater than both Jonah and Solomon was now amongst them.

A Pharisee invited Him to eat and was wondering why Jesus did not wash before the meal. Jesus said that the Pharisees were fools who cleaned the outside of a plate or cup while they were rotten inside. They had better show kindness from the inside, and everything would be clean for them. They always get the best of everything while riding on others, and the lawyers use the law to their advantage while others suffer. They have built monuments to their fathers' works, which means that they approve of the killings and bad deeds that their fathers did. They would all be charged by God for what they did. The Pharisees tried to trap Him into saying something wrong, but they couldn't.

Jesus told His disciples that they should fear the One who has power to cast into hell and not the one who kills the body. Everything is taken into account by God. Whoever acknowledges Him here on earth will be acknowledged by God in the presence of His angels. Whoever says anything against Him can be forgiven but whoever blasphemes against the Holy Spirit will never be forgiven. They should not worry if they have problems with the rulers and authorities because the Holy Spirit would guide them and tell them what to say.

When someone in the crowd asked Jesus to tell his brother to share his inheritance with him, Jesus said it was not up to

Him but that they should watch out against greed, for a man's life is not made up of the abundance of his possessions.

Jesus then told the parable of the man who had so much wealth he did not know what to do with it, so he decided to eat, drink, and enjoy himself. But he was a fool because God would take his soul from him immediately. That is what happens to those who store up treasures but are not rich in relation to God. For this reason, Jesus said that they should never worry about what they would eat or wear, for life is more than nourishment, and the body more than clothes.

God feeds even the ravens who don't sow or even own a barn, so how much more a human being? God looks after everybody and everything, so they should never worry, because He is pleased to give them His Kingdom.

They should sell what they have and give it to charity because one's heart will always be where one's treasure is. Be like persons who wait for their master when he comes home from a wedding, ever ready to open the doors for him. Happy are those slaves whom the master finds alert when he returns. One should be ready because the Son of Man (Day of Redemption) would come when one least expects Him to. Anyone who knows what to do and doesn't do it will be punished. One knows how to tell if it is going to rain by the clouds, so how come one cannot tell when the end is coming? Those who cannot see this are hypocrites.

If you owe someone money, try to pay him before he reports you and you end up in prison. It's the same with Judgement Day. Try to repent and change before that day comes. People who have suffered like the eighteen on whom the Siloam tower fell and killed, had not committed any greater sin than the rest of Jerusalem, but unless one repents, he will perish in the same way.

Jesus told them the parable of the man who owned the fig tree that did not bear fruit for three years. He told his farmer to cut it down, but the farmer pleaded with him to give the tree one more chance and he would put fertilizer on it and maybe it would grow the next year, but if not, he would cut it down. Jesus then healed a woman who for eighteen years could not walk straight. She was made erect, and she praised God.

When the ruler of the synagogue complained about Jesus healing on the Sabbath, Jesus called him a hypocrite and said, *"Doesn't everyone release his animals and take them out to drink on the Sabbath? Why then should this woman not be released on the Sabbath?"* Jesus then said that the Kingdom of God was like a mustard seed that a man planted in his garden. It grew up into a tree, and the birds made nests in its branches. It was also like yeast that a woman took and mixed in three batches of flour until it was all raised.

Jesus made His way into Jerusalem and was asked whether only a few people would be saved. Jesus said that they should strain every nerve to enter through the narrow door, for many will try to enter and will be unable to. You will try to knock, but He will not answer you and will tell you to go away because you are evil doers. You will cry when you see Abraham, Isaac, Jacob, and all the angels sitting with God and you are kept outside.

When told by certain Pharisees to leave the area because Herod wanted to kill Him, Jesus told them to tell Herod that He was going to expel demons and cure people that very day and the next. He would complete His work on the third day.

Jesus went for a meal with one of the Pharisee leaders on the Sabbath and cured a man who had dropsy. When questioned, Jesus replied that if someone's donkey or ox falls into a pit on the Sabbath, wouldn't he pull it out? Jesus said whoever makes himself prominent will be humbled and whoever humbles himself will be set high. When inviting people to dinner, only invite the poor, lame, blind, or maimed because they have nothing to repay you. Your reward will be at the resurrection of the just.

Jesus told the parable of the man who gave a great supper and invited many friends who all made excuses and failed to show up. So the man sent his slaves to go out and bring the maimed, blind, and the lame off the streets until his house was full. Jesus said that whoever comes to Him without hating his family and himself cannot be his disciple. Likewise whoever does not carry his own cross and come after Him cannot be His disciple. Whoever cannot part with all he has can also not be His disciple.

When Jesus was asked why He mixed and ate with sinners and tax collectors, He asked them who would not be happy if he had a hundred sheep and one got lost but was later found? There is more joy in Heaven for one repentant sinner than the ninety-nine righteous persons who do not need repentance. Even a woman, who has ten silver coins, loses one, and later finds it, is happy and will tell her friends to rejoice with her over the lost coin that was found.

This made Jesus tell the parable of the prodigal son who took his share of his inheritance from his father and left the house. He squandered the money on reckless living and ended up being hired to tend the pigs in the field. A severe famine came, and he was very hungry. Regretting what he had done, he decided to go back home and repent to his father.

His father saw him on his way home, ran up to him, kissed him, gave him new clothes, and put a ring on his finger. When he told his father that he was sorry and was not fit to be called his son, the father ordered his servants to kill a calf and throw a party because his lost son had been found.

The man's elder son was annoyed that such attention should be showered on his brother and refused to go to the party. He said he'd worked many years for his father and he had never thrown a party for him. The father replied that he was always with him and what he had was his, but his brother was dead and had come to life. He was lost and had been found.

Jesus told His disciples the parable of the rich man who was about to sack his dishonest manager who went and reduced the debts of his master's debtors. The master rather commended his dishonest manager for acting shrewdly. Jesus said that one should use unrighteous wealth to win friends who, when things fail, may welcome you and look after you forever. He who is faithful in little things will also be faithful in big things, and he who is unreliable with very little will be unreliable with much. If you are not reliable with what belongs to someone else, who will give you anything for your personal possession? No slave can serve two masters as he will love one more than the other, likewise one cannot serve both God and money. The Pharisees, lovers of money, started laughing at Jesus, but He called them hypocrites because God knew what was in their hearts.

Jesus continued by saying that what seems outstanding to men is abhorrent in the sight of God. Whoever divorces his wife and marries another, commits adultery. It is the same with the man who marries a divorcee.

Jesus told the parable of the rich man who refused to help Lazarus, a beggar who finally died and went to Heaven. The rich man also died but went to hell and saw Lazarus in Heaven but could not come in. In life, Lazarus had the bad things, and so his reward was in Heaven. If your brother sins, call him to task, and if he repents, forgive him, no matter how many times he sins, so long as he always says sorry. When the disciples asked Jesus to give them more faith, He told them to do their duty without asking for a reward.

Jesus then cleansed some lepers on His way to Jerusalem. Only one of them came and thanked God, and Jesus told him that his faith had saved him. When the Pharisees asked Jesus when the Kingdom of God would come, Jesus said that it did not come by looking for it, but it was already in their midst. The end of the world would come suddenly just as in the days of Noah, and everybody would be destroyed. Whoever tries to preserve his life would lose it, and whoever loses it will preserve it alive.

Jesus told them to always pray and not lose courage. He told them the parable of the judge who decided to treat a woman with justice because she kept bothering him, even though the judge was a hard unfeeling man who did not believe in God. How much more would God do to those faithful ones who pray to Him!

Jesus told another parable of the Pharisee and the tax collector who both went to pray. The Pharisee thanked God for not being like other men who were thieves, cheats, and adulterers. The tax collector simply said, *"God be merciful to me, the sinner."* He was the one forgiven by God. He who exalts himself will be humbled, but he who humbles himself will be exalted. Jesus told them to allow the children to come to Him, saying that unless one receives the Kingdom of God like a child, he cannot get in.

One of the rulers asked Jesus what he had to do to inherit eternal life. Jesus told him to obey the Commandments. When the man claimed that he had done so all his life, Jesus told him to sell everything, donate it to the poor, and follow Him because he would have riches in Heaven. The man went away very sad because he was a rich man. Jesus said it was easier for a camel to pass through the eye of a needle than for a rich man to enter the Kingdom of God. Anyone who gives up anything for God will receive it ten times over and will have eternal life.

Jesus then told His disciples that He would soon be betrayed, handed over to the Gentiles, ridiculed, insulted, spat on, flogged, and finally executed. However, He would rise up again on the third day.

Jesus cured a blind man on the outskirts of Jericho who had pleaded with Him to cure him, calling Him *"Son of David."* Jesus said his faith had saved him, and he regained his sight. All the people gave praise to God.

Jesus went into Jericho, saw Zacchaeus, a wealthy tax collector, who had climbed into a tree because he was too short to see Him. Jesus told him He was going to his house. When the crowd complained that he was a sinner, Zacchaeus told Jesus that he would give away half of his property to the poor. Jesus said that he had been saved from that day.

Jesus told the parable of the rich man who went away and gave ten of his slaves the equivalent of twenty dollars each to trade with. The townsmen did not like him and sent a delegation after him to tell him that they did not want him to be king over them.

On his return, one slave had made two hundred dollars from his twenty dollars and was put in charge of ten cities. Another had made one hundred dollars from his twenty dollars and was put in charge of five cities. One of them came and returned his twenty dollars, claiming that he was afraid to touch it because he knew his boss was a harsh thief who reaped what he did not sow. The rich man took his twenty dollars and gave it to the man who had made the two hundred dollars. He then executed the townsmen who had complained about him. So Jesus said, likewise God will give to the one who has, but can also take from the one who has not, everything he has.

Jesus then sent some messengers to get Him a colt, and He rode on it. The people spread their clothes on the road in front of Him. As He approached the Mount of Olives, they all started singing praises to Him, *"Blessed be the King who comes in God's Name! Peace in Heaven and glory in the highest!"*

Jesus wept when He saw the city of Jerusalem because He knew that one day all of it would be destroyed. He threw out the traders in the Temple saying it was a house of prayer and not for robbers. He was teaching in the Temple while the chief priests, scribes, and leaders of the people were plotting to destroy Him.

One day as He was teaching, the chief priests asked Him by whose authority He was teaching. Jesus asked them by whose authority was John the Baptist teaching, and they thought it was a trap, so they said that they did not know. Jesus then replied that He would also not tell them by whose authority He was teaching.

Jesus then told the parable of a man who planted a vineyard and leased it to his tenants. When he sent his slaves to collect his share, they beat them and threw them out on three occasions, so he sent his son, who was killed. The owner would obviously come and destroy the tenants and give the vineyard to others. So Jesus said, the stone the builders rejected had become the chief stone of the corner. Whoever falls on that stone will be crushed, and whoever the stone falls on will be destroyed.

The chief priests wanted to destroy Jesus right there and then but were restrained by the crowd. They had realized that the parable was about them. They plotted to catch Him saying something wrong so that they could hand Him over to the governor. So they asked Jesus whether it was right to pay tax to Caesar. Jesus asked for a coin, which had Caesar's head on it, and said that they should pay to Caesar what belonged to Caesar and to God what belonged to God.

The Sadducees, who don't believe in resurrection, asked Jesus what would happen if a woman's husband died and as was customary, she was given to his brother to wed, who also died and so on until she had had seven husbands. Whose wife would she be in Heaven? Jesus said that the relationships of this life were necessary because here people die and need to be replaced. There is no need for marriage in Heaven for there is no death there. Jesus went on to show that there is life after death by pointing to what God had said to Moses in the passage of the burning bush, that He was the God of Abraham, Isaac and Jacob (Exodus 3). He is not the God of the dead but of the living, because to Him we are all alive.

The scribes praised Jesus because they were afraid to ask Him any more questions. People had complained about Jesus using a title they felt was too exalted for Him (Son of David). Jesus replied saying that such a title does not say too much but too little for David himself calls Him (not son but) Lord in the book of Psalms saying, "*The Lord said to my Lord, Be seated at My right until I make Your enemies a footstool for Your feet*" (Psalm 110). Jesus then told the crowd to beware of the scribes who walk around in long robes and love salutations in public places and front seats in the synagogues and banquets. They would receive a severer sentence.

When Jesus saw a poor widow putting in two copper coins into the treasury, Jesus said that she had put in more than all the rich men, because she had given all that she had.

Jesus pointed to the beautiful Temple and told the disciples that all that would soon be destroyed. But they should be careful that they were not misled because many people would come in His Name saying, "*I am He, and the Time is near.*" They should not listen to them or take notice when wars and disturbances happen because they must first come before the end, which would not come immediately.

Nations will rise against nations, and there will be earthquakes, famines, plagues, and horrors. All are signs from Heaven. They the disciples themselves would be persecuted, imprisoned, and made to suffer because of Him, but He will tell them what to say, and no one will be able to refute them. They will be hated by everyone for confessing Him, but nothing will happen to them, and they will gain possession of their souls.

They will know that the end is pending when they see Jerusalem surrounded by armies. It will be the day of vengeance in fulfilment of all that had been written. Jerusalem will be destroyed by Gentiles until their period is completed. There will also be signs in the sun, the moon, the stars, the seas, and the waves. Then they will see the Son of Man coming in a cloud with great power and glory. But when these things happen, they should hold their heads up high because their deliverance is near.

Like a fig tree, one knows when they are fully budding that summer is near. Likewise, when they notice the signs, they will know that the Kingdom of God is near. Heaven and earth will pass away, but His words will not pass away. They should be strong and pray so that they may escape the impending events and stand in God's presence.

Jesus taught in the Temple during the day and went to the Mount of Olives at night to pray.

As the feast of the Passover approached, the chief priests and the scribes plotted to kill Jesus. Satan entered Judas Iscariot, and he went and made a deal with them to betray Jesus for money.

On the day of Unleavened Bread when the Passover was to be sacrificed, Jesus sent Peter and John to meet up with a man carrying a pitcher of water who was to show them the room in which they were to eat the Passover supper. Jesus said that it would be the last time He would eat with them before He was made to suffer.

He took a cup, gave thanks, and told the disciples to divide it amongst themselves because He would never drink wine again until the coming of the Kingdom of God. He took some bread, gave thanks, and broke it, saying it was His Body and they should eat it in His memory. Likewise He took the cup and said it was His Blood and they should drink it in His memory. Jesus stated that there was somebody at the table who would betray Him.

When the disciples started arguing amongst themselves as to which one of them was the most important, Jesus said the most prominent must be the youngest and the leader is the one who serves. All of them would be finally honoured in Heaven sitting on thrones judging the twelve tribes of Israel. Peter told Jesus that He was ready to go to prison and die for Him, but Jesus replied that he would deny Him three times before the cock crowed that day.

Jesus went to the Mount of Olives, and His disciples followed Him. Jesus prayed hard for strength. When He returned, He found the disciples sleeping.

Suddenly a mob led by Judas appeared, and he came forward to kiss Jesus. Jesus asked Judas if he was betraying him with a kiss. One of the disciples cut off the right ear of one of the high priest's slaves. Jesus told them to stop and healed the man's ear. Jesus asked the priests why they did not arrest him when He was preaching in the Temple and have now come with clubs and swords as if He were a robber. They arrested Jesus and took Him to the high priest's house where he was blindfolded and ridiculed.

On three occasions, three different women asked Peter if he was one of Jesus' followers, and each time he denied it. Suddenly the cock crowed, and Peter remembered what Jesus had said, and he went outside and started crying.

At the break of day, they took Jesus to the tribunal and asked Him if He was the Christ. He said He would from then on be seated at the right hand of God Almighty. When asked if He was the Son of God, He replied, *"You say I am."* The priests agreed that they now had enough proof to convict Him. They took Him to Pilate, saying that He had refused to pay taxes to Caesar and He called Himself The Messiah.

When Pilate asked Him if this were true, Jesus then said, *"You say so."* Pilate said that he found nothing wrong with Him, but the chief priests insisted that He was a trouble-maker and a Galilean, whereby Pilate sent Jesus to Herod as He was under his jurisdiction

Herod was pleased to see Jesus and even wanted Him to perform a miracle. Jesus, however, kept quiet and never an-swered any of his questions. They changed Jesus' clothes and took Him back to Pilate. Herod and Pilate on that day became friends, as they had been enemies before.

Pilate told the mob that he could find nothing wrong in Jesus and would flog Him and let Him go. The crowd, knowing that it was customary to release one prisoner on the festival day, shouted to Pilate to release Barabbas, the most notorious criminal and murderer of the day, and cru-cify Jesus. Pilate then released Barabbas and handed Jesus over to them. They took Him to a place called the "Skull" with two other robbers carrying crosses. They got a Cyre-nian called Simon to carry Jesus' cross.

Jesus told the women who were crying and following Him not to cry for Him but rather for themselves and their chil-dren, because a time would come when people would say, *"Happy are the childless."* The three of them were crucified, and Jesus said, *"Father, forgive them for they do not know what they are doing."*

The crowd divided His clothes among themselves by cast-ing lots. They wrote, *"This is the King of the Jews"* on the top of His cross. They laughed at Him, giving Him vinegar to drink, and said that He had saved others, but He could not save Himself. One robber told Jesus to save them, and the other said that they at least deserved to be crucified, but Jesus had done nothing wrong. He then asked Jesus to remember him when He entered into His Kingdom. Jesus assured him that they would be together that very day in Paradise.

At midday there was darkness everywhere for three hours, and the veil of the Temple was torn in two. In a loud voice Jesus cried, *"Father into Your hands I commend My Spirit"* and died. The centurion who saw everything praised God and said, *"Truly this man was innocent."* The crowd observed everything from a distance.

A certain man called Joseph of Arimathea went to Pilate to ask for Jesus' body, which he took down, wrapped in linen, and put into a tomb made of rock. The women who had accompanied Jesus from Galilee, followed His body to the tomb and went home to prepare spices and perfume to put on His body. When they returned a couple of days later, they found the stone rolled away from the tomb, and the body of Jesus had disappeared. Two men in dazzling clothes told them that Jesus had risen as He said He would. The women, (Mary Magdalene, Joanna, and Mary the mother of James) went and told the disciples what they had seen. The disciples did not believe them, but Peter ran to the tomb and confirmed what the women had said.

Two apostles were walking to a village called Emmaus, and Jesus appeared to them, but they did not recognise Him. One of them, Cleopas, thought He was a stranger and told Him how the chief priests had caused the crucifixion of one Jesus of Nazareth, a mighty prophet who had come to deliver Israel, and all that had happened up until the disappearance of the body. Jesus reprimanded them for having so little faith in the scriptures and what they had said about Him.

As it was getting late, they urged Him not to go on alone but to stay the night with them. During dinner, they finally recognised Him, but He quickly disappeared.

They went and told the disciples that Jesus had indeed risen. They were relating their experience to them when Jesus Himself appeared. The disciples were frightened, thinking they had seen a ghost, but He told them to touch Him, and He showed them His hands and feet. They gave

Him some fish to eat, and He told them that all He had said before had now come true. He was to suffer, die, and rise again on the third day and repentance leading to forgiveness should be preached in His Name to all nations.

He walked with them as far as Bethany, and He blessed them and disappeared to Heaven. They worshipped him and returned to Jerusalem with great joy, constantly praising God in the Temple.

THE GOSPEL ACCORDING TO JOHN

"In the beginning was the Word and the Word was with God, and the Word was God. Through Him, everything came into being and without Him nothing that exists came into being. In Him was Life, and the Life was the Light of men." John the Baptist was sent by God to be a witness to testify about the Light that was coming into the world. His own people did not receive Him, but to those who did receive Him, He granted authority to become God's children. That is, those who owe everything to God. John testified about Him, saying that this was the One whom he had been talking about, One who is greater than he and ranks ahead of him because He was before him. The Law was given through Moses but grace and truth came through Jesus Christ. No one had ever seen God, but His only begotten Son, Jesus Christ, has made Him known.

The Jews sent priests and levites to ask John who he thought he was by baptising people, and he replied that he baptised with water only, but there was someone amongst them, whom they did not recognise, who would come after him and be much greater than he. This happened in Bethany where John was baptising.

The next day he saw Jesus approaching and told everyone that here was the Lamb of God, the One he had been talking about and that He was the Son of God.

Simon Peter and his brother Andrew followed Jesus to listen to Him. Jesus changed Simon Peter's name to Cephas, which meant Peter. Later, Philip and Nathaniel also followed Jesus.

Two days later at a wedding, Jesus turned six large jars of water into wine when it had run out. He did not tell anyone what He had done, although the servants, His disciples, and

His mother knew. This happened in Cana, a town in Galilee, and His disciples believed in Him.

Jesus then went to Jerusalem and threw out all the people who were trading and dealing in the Temple. He overturned all the tables and used a whip to throw out the animals and people, saying that they should not do that in His Father's house. When questioned by the Jews about the authority He had for clearing the Temple, Jesus replied that if they were to destroy the Temple, which had taken forty-six years to build, He would rebuild it in three days. But Jesus was actually talking about His bodily temple, and the disciples remembered it after Jesus had died and rose again.

One of the Jewish rulers, a Pharisee called Nicodemus, was told by Jesus that unless a man is born from above, he cannot see the Kingdom of God. When Nicodemus asked Him how a man could be born when he was old, Jesus replied that unless one's birth is through water and the spirit, he cannot enter the Kingdom of God. What is born of the flesh is flesh, and what is born of the spirit is spirit. As one cannot see the wind, one cannot also see the spirit.

Jesus castigated Nicodemus that as a teacher he should have known these things. How is he expected to believe anything that He says concerning heavenly things? For God so loved the world that He gave His only begotten Son, so that whoever believes in Him should not perish, but have everlasting life. For God did not send His Son into the world to condemn the world but in order that the world through Him might be saved. He who believes in Him will never be condemned. He who does not believe is already condemned. Those who practise evil, hate the light and love the darkness, because they don't want their activities to be exposed.

Jesus and His disciples went to the Judean countryside where they baptised. John also was baptising at Aenon, and when some of John's followers complained to him about Jesus baptising, John confirmed that Jesus was sent from Heaven and was greater than he. Anyone who accepts His testimony attests that God is true. He who believes in the

Son has eternal life; he who disobeys the Son will not see life, but God's anger will remain on him.

In actual fact, Jesus did not baptise; it was His disciples, but when the Pharisees heard about it, Jesus went to Sychar, passing through Samaria where He asked a Samaritan woman, who came to draw water, to give Him some to drink. The woman asked Him how He a Jew should ask her for a drink. Jesus replied that if she really knew who He was, and knew God's gift, she would have asked for living water. When she asked Him how she could get the living water, Jesus said that whoever drinks from the living water will never thirst again. He told her correctly that she had had five husbands and was currently living with one out of wedlock.

He also told her that salvation came from the Jews and that God was looking for people who will worship Him in spirit and in truth, because God was a Spirit. Jesus told her He was the Messiah whom she had heard about. When His disciples came, she went off to tell her people that she had seen the Christ.

Jesus did not eat when offered food by His disciples, saying that His nourishment came from doing God's will and work. He told the disciples that He sent them to reap a crop on which they had not worked. Because of the woman, Jesus stayed for two days, and the Samaritans were converted, believing Him to be the Saviour of the world. He then went to Galilee, saying that a prophet had no honour in his native country. The Galileans welcomed Him.

Jesus went to Cana, the place where He had changed water into wine, and told a courtier whose son lay ill in Capernaum he should go home that his son would live. When told that his son had got up at exactly the time that Jesus had said, this man's entire household became believers.

Jesus went to Jerusalem and healed a paralysed man who had been ill for thirty-eight years. This was beside a bathing pool called Bethzath in Hebrew, where all the invalids used to bathe and become cured of their ailments after an angel had stirred the water. Being paralysed, the man could never get into the water. Because Jesus had done this on the Sabbath, the Jews persecuted Him when the paralysed man told them who had cured him. They were more determined to kill Him when he referred to God as His Father, because that made Him equal to God.

Jesus said that whoever does not honour the Son, does not honour the Father who sent Him. He who listens to His Message and believes in the One who sent Him will come under no sentence but will be passed over from death into life. The time was coming when only those who hear will live. Those who have practised evil will be condemned.

Jesus continued by saying that He was not acting on His own but that everything He did was the will of the One who sent Him. What John the Baptist had testified about Him was all true.

Jesus castigated them for believing the scriptures and thinking that they would have eternal life, but He was the One they should listen to because He came in His Father's Name. How could they enjoy praise from each other but not seek praise from the One and Only God? Moses had even written about Him. If they did not believe Moses' writings then how would they believe His teachings?

Jesus then went to the other side of the Sea of Galilee (or the Sea of Tiberias) followed by a huge crowd. He used five barley cakes and two fish to feed the crowd of more than five thousand people. The remains filled twelve baskets.

Jesus withdrew to the mountains when He realised that some of them knew that He was the prophet they had all heard about and wanted to kill Him.

The disciples went in a boat to sea, and a strong wind rocked the boat. They saw Jesus walking on the water towards them, and He calmed the waves.

The crowds went into boats and followed Jesus, who reprimanded them for following for purely material reasons, following because they were fed after His miracle with the bread and fish. Jesus said that they should work not for perishable food but rather for the food of eternal life, such as what He would teach them.

The people asked Him what they had to do to accomplish God's works and to show them a sign so that they would believe in Him. Jesus said that whatever comes down from Heaven and furnishes life to the world is the Bread of God. Jesus continued by saying that He was the Bread of Life. He who comes to Him will never be hungry, and he who believes in Him will never thirst.

He will never reject anyone who comes to Him because He came to do God's will and not His own. He who believes in Him will have eternal life. He who eats His Flesh and drinks His Blood will have eternal life. All this happened when He was preaching in a synagogue at Capernaum.

When He heard the disciples grumbling, Jesus said that the Spirit was the life giver, and the flesh did not benefit at all. His words were spirit and life, but some of them failed to believe Him. Jesus already knew who the disbelievers were and who would betray Him, so He said no one could come to Him unless it was granted to him by His Father.

From then on, many of His disciples stopped walking with Him, but the twelve were left. Jesus asked them why they did not go too, and they confirmed their faith in Him. Jesus then said that one of them was a devil. He meant Judas Iscariot who was going to betray Him.

Jesus went around Galilee because He did not want to go near Judea as the Jews were looking to kill Him. At the Jewish Feast of the Booths, Jesus sent His disciples instead and went quietly by Himself to observe the people. They were all looking for Him, arguing amongst themselves whether He was good or bad.

Jesus then went to the Temple to preach and the people were amazed as to how He knew the Scriptures without any education. Jesus replied that His teachings were all words from the One who sent Him. Anyone who willed to do His Will would understand the teaching. He who speaks for himself seeks his own honour, and only he who seeks to honour the One who sent Him is sincere.

They were shocked when Jesus asked them why they wanted to kill Him and why they complained that He healed people on the Sabbath when they themselves circumcised people on the Sabbath. They should not be hypocrites. People were amazed that He was brave enough to be talking amongst those who planned to kill Him.

The Pharisees sent people to arrest Him, and Jesus said He would be with them a little while longer before going back to the One who sent Him. This confused His enemies because they did not know what He was talking about.

On the final day of the feast, Jesus asked those who were thirsty to come and drink, saying that whoever believed in Him would never thirst because streams of water would flow from his innermost being. He said this meaning the Spirit, whom those who believed in Him were about to receive, for as yet the Spirit had not been given because Jesus was not glorified.

The people sent to arrest Jesus returned to the Pharisees to say that they could not touch him because no one ever spoke the way He did. Nicodemus confirmed that the law could not condemn a man without giving him a hearing.

The Pharisees brought an adulteress to Jesus, saying Moses had written that she should be stoned. Jesus wrote something on the ground and asked those who had not sinned to throw the first stone. They all left except the woman. Jesus told her to go and not sin again, as there was no one left to accuse her.

Jesus told the Pharisees that He was the Light of the world and He had a right to judge and testify for Himself because He was not alone but was working for the One who sent Him. He told them that they did not know Him or His Father. They would die in their sin, and where He was going, none of them could go. He said that He was not from their world and that nothing He did was of His own accord, but He did everything as His Father wanted.

Those who believed in Him would become His disciples and be free. Even though they claimed to be Abraham's offspring, they were still looking for ways to kill Him. If God was truly their Father then they would love Him and not go against Him. They still had the devil in them and that is why they could not bear to listen to Him. Anyone who observes His teaching will not see death.

The Jews retorted that even Abraham and the prophets died, so who was He to glorify Himself? Jesus replied that He came before Abraham, and He knew God and they didn't. They picked up stones to throw at Him, but Jesus hid and escaped out of the Temple.

On His way out, Jesus saw a blind man and explained to the disciples that it was not because he or his parents had sinned that the man was blind, but it was in him that God's works were displayed. He spat on some mud, put it on the man's eyes, and told him to go and wash his eyes in the pool at Siloam (which means Sent). The man did that and regained his sight.

He went and told everyone that Jesus had cured him, and they brought him to the Pharisees who could not agree whether Jesus was good or bad. Some blamed Him for healing on the Sabbath, and others asked how a sinner could heal anybody. They asked the man's parents, who, afraid of being barred from the synagogue by the Jews for confessing Christ, told them to ask the man himself if he had been born blind. The man told them that Jesus was obviously from God otherwise He would not have been able to give him his sight.

They expelled him, and he met Jesus again who asked him if he believed in the Son of Man. The man said he believed and worshipped Jesus.

Jesus told the Pharisees that sin remained in those who had sight but the blind were blameless. Jesus said that just as sheep will only listen to the voice of their shepherd, a thief would never go through the door. He, Jesus, was the door, and whoever comes through Him will be saved. The good shepherd lays down his life for his sheep, but a hired hand who does not own the sheep will run when he sees the wolf coming. He is the good shepherd who will lay down His life in order that He may take it up again. For this reason, His Father loves Him and gives Him the authority to lay down and take up His life again.

During the Feast of Dedication, the Jews surrounded Jesus in the Temple and asked Him to tell them if He was really the Christ. Jesus said that He had already told them through His works but they had not believed Him, which meant that they did not belong to His sheep who all had eternal life given to them by His Father, and that He and His Father were the same.

When they picked up stones to throw at Him for blaspheming, Jesus said that they were the ones who were blaspheming because His Father sent Him to accomplish a job, and they did not believe Him. If they believed what He had done, then they would know that His Father was in Him and He in His Father. They tried to grab Him, but Jesus escaped and went to a place beyond the Jordan where John first baptised and continued His teaching.

Jesus heard that Lazarus, the brother of Mary and Martha, had died and had been buried for four days. He and His disciples went to Bethany to the house. Jesus asked Martha if she really believed in Him, and she said that she had faith that He was the Christ and the Son of God. Jesus said He was the Resurrection and the Life. He who believed in Him would live even when he had died, and he who lived and believed in Him would never die. Martha and Mary took Jesus to Lazarus' tomb, and He raised him up from the dead.

The people who saw this miracle went and told the Pharisees, who convened a meeting and made plans to kill Jesus, because they did not want the people believing too much in Him. It would give the Romans an opportunity to invade them and take away their holy place.

Jesus no longer went around openly and withdrew near the wilderness to a town called Ephraim. The chief priests sent out an order for Jesus to be arrested on sight.

Jesus had dinner at Simon the leper's house, where Mary wiped His feet with her hair using an expensive perfume. Judas Iscariot complained that it was a waste of money because the perfume could have been sold and given to the poor. (He said this because he was a thief. He was in charge of the money bag and always pilfered the collections belonging to the group.) Jesus told him to allow her to use the perfume for the day of His burial. The poor would always be there, but He would not.

The chief priests planned to kill Lazarus as well because were it not for his being raised from the dead, Jesus would not have so many believers.

The next day Jesus rode into Jerusalem on a donkey, and a huge crowd followed Him shouting, *"Hosanna! Blessed is He who comes in the Name of the Lord!"* and singing His praises. It was only after Jesus was glorified that the disciples remembered this incident was to do with what was written in the Scriptures, *"Have no fear, daughter of Zion. Behold, your king is coming, seated on an ass's colt"* (Zechariah 9:9).

Jesus told His disciples that whoever loves his life will lose it, but the one who hates his life in this world will preserve it to eternal life. If anyone serves Him, the Father will honour him. The time had come for Him to be glorified. A voice suddenly came from Heaven saying, *"I have glorified it, and I will glorify it again."* This was after Jesus had asked God to glorify His Name.

The people who heard the voice were all amazed. Jesus said that when He would be lifted up from the earth, He would draw everyone to Himself. He was talking about His death. They should all put faith in the Light, because He was the Light. Anyone who walks in darkness does not know where he is going.

A lot of people believed in Jesus but were afraid the Pharisees would throw them out of the synagogue if they showed any inclination towards Him.

Jesus said that he who believed in Him and saw Him also believed and saw the Father because they are the same, and He is the Light that has come to light up the world. He did not come to judge the world but to save it, so whoever did not believe in Him will have his judge for He will not pass sentence on him. His spoken word will judge him on the last day. His Father had given Him a command, which is eternal life, and He had come to do His Father's Will.

Before the Passover feast, Jesus, aware that He would soon leave this world and go to the Father, washed the feet of His disciples and dried them with a towel during supper. He knew that the devil had already turned the heart of Judas Iscariot to betray Him, so He said that not all of them were clean. He had set an example to them by washing their feet even though He was their Teacher. A slave is not superior to his master.

Jesus said He knew those whom He had chosen, but the Scripture had to be fulfilled. One of them would betray Him. So Jesus dipped a piece of bread and gave it to Judas Iscariot, telling him to do what he had to do quickly. Judas went out, but none of the disciples knew why.

Jesus then said He was now glorified, and God was glorified in Him. They should love one another as He had loved them, so that everyone will recognise that they are His disciples. Peter asked Him where He was going and told Him he would lay down his life for Him. Jesus replied that he would betray Him three times before the rooster crowed.

Jesus said He was going to prepare a place for them in Heaven. He is the Way, the Truth, and the Life and no one comes to the Father except through Him. "*I am in the Father and the Father in Me,*" said Jesus when Philip asked Him to show them the Father.

Jesus continued by saying that the one who believed in Him, would do greater works than He did because He was going away. He would do whatever they asked in His Name. If they loved Him, they should keep His Commandments. He who observes His orders loves Him, and he who loves Him will be loved by the Father and Him. He would always be inside the one who loves Him. The Holy Spirit will teach them everything and will remind them all that He has told them, so that when it does happen they will have faith and know that He loves the Father and therefore do everything He has asked them to do.

Jesus said He was the Vine and they were the branches. A branch cannot bear fruit unless it is on a vine therefore they also could not do anything if they did not remain with Him. No one has greater love than to lay down his life for his friends. They are His friends because He chose them; they did not choose Him. So He has appointed them to go and spread the Message and do His work in His Name. They should love one another. This was His Commandment to them. If the world hates them they should remember that it hated Him first. They will be hated and persecuted on account of Him because those who hate Him do not know the One who sent Him. People would not have been guilty if He had not come and spoken to them, but now they have no excuse. He who hates Him hates His Father as well.

All that has happened is in fulfilment of the Law. People have hated Him without just cause. They (the disciples) will testify for Him because they were with Him from the beginning. It will come to a point that whoever kills them will think he is doing a service to God. But Jesus continued by saying that He was telling them these things so that when the time would come, they would remember that He told them first. When the Judgement Day comes, God will come and convict the world regarding sin, righteousness, and judgement because the world did not believe in Him.

Jesus said that in a little while, they would not see Him, and again in a little while, they would see Him, meaning that at first they would be sad when He was gone but their sadness would later turn to joy. Because they had loved Him and believed that He came from the Father, God would also love them. They would have peace in Him.

Jesus then raised His eyes towards Heaven and asked God to glorify Him because He had completed the task that He had been given. He had made His (God's) Name known to the people whom He (God) had given Him from the world. Jesus asked God to look after them because they now belonged to Him, as He was now leaving them. He also asked God to look after all those who also believed in Him. Jesus said that He would love those whom God had given Him to be with Him, so that they may see the glory that God had given Him.

Jesus and His disciples then went across the Kidron Brook to a garden where Judas Iscariot was waiting with some soldiers. Jesus asked them who they were looking for and when they said Jesus of Nazareth, He admitted He was the One. Peter cut off the ear of one of the high priest's slaves with a sword, but Jesus told him to put his sword away. The slave's name was Malchus.

They tied up Jesus and took Him to Annas, the father-in-law of the chief priest Caiaphas. Annas asked Jesus about His teachings, but He replied that He had been teaching all the time in the Temple and not in secret, so why should he now ask Him about it? One of the attendants slapped Him for being insolent to a high priest.

Meanwhile Peter was asked on three occasions whether he was one of the disciples. When he denied it for the third time, the cock crowed. Jesus was sent, still tied up, from Annas to Caiaphas to Pontius Pilate who asked the Jews what He had done wrong. They replied that if Jesus was not a criminal, they would not have sent Him to him. Pilate told them to go and sentence Him according to their law. The priests replied that they did not have the power to execute anyone.

Pilate then privately asked Jesus if He was the King of the Jews. Jesus asked him if he was asking of his own accord or had the others told him to ask that. Pilate replied that he was not a Jew. Jesus said that His Kingdom was not of this world. Pilate asked Him if He was a king, and Jesus replied, *"You say that I am a king. I was born and entered the world that I might testify to the truth."*

Pilate asked Him, *"What is truth?"* Then he went out and told the Jews that he did not find Jesus guilty, but as it was their custom to free a prisoner at the Passover, should he then free the King of the Jews? The Jews replied that he should free Barabbas the robber instead.

Pilate then had Jesus flogged, and the soldiers put a crown of thorns on His head and dressed Him in a purple robe. They slapped Him and said, "*Long live the King of the Jews.*" Pilate told them to take Jesus and crucify Him themselves if they wanted, but he did not find Him guilty. The Jews said that He should die because he made Himself out to be God's Son.

Pilate again asked Jesus where He was from, and Jesus refused to answer. When Pilate told Him that he had the power to free Him or crucify Him, Jesus said that the only power he had came from above, and the one who betrayed Him had greater sin than he.

Pilate wanted to free Him, but the Jews said that anyone who made himself out to be a king, rebelled against Caesar. Pilate then asked the Jews whether he should crucify Him, and the crowd shouted, "*Crucify Him!*" Pilate was a coward and handed Jesus over to be crucified.

Jesus was led out, carrying His cross, to the Skull (Golgotha in Hebrew) where they crucified Him. They wrote on His cross, "*JESUS, THE NAZARENE, THE KING OF THE JEWS.*" The priests even wanted to change the writing to "*THIS MAN CLAIMED TO BE THE KING OF THE JEWS,*" but Pilate refused saying, "*What I have written, I have written.*"

After crucifying Him, the soldiers took His clothes, divided them into four, and drew lots to share them. Jesus' mother, His aunt Mary (wife of Clopas), and Mary Magdalene were by the cross. Jesus told John, His disciple, that Mary, His mother, was now his mother and he, her son.

Jesus said He was thirsty, so they soaked a sponge in vinegar and held it up to His mouth. Jesus then said, "*It is finished,*" bowed His head, and died.

Jesus had been crucified with two others. The Jews then asked Pilate not to leave the bodies on the cross over the Sabbath, so they came to break the legs of those on the cross to hasten their death. However, Jesus was already dead.

One of the soldiers pierced His side with a spear and blood and water came out. These things happened in order for the scriptures to be carried out.

Joseph of Arimathea asked Pilate's permission to remove Jesus' body. He and Nicodemus took Jesus' body and wrapped it up in linen and spices, as was the Jewish custom for burial. They put Him in a tomb close by.

Mary Magdalene came on the Sunday after the crucifixion to Jesus' tomb and found that the stone had been moved. She ran to tell Peter and another disciple. They all ran to the tomb and saw only Jesus' clothes inside.

Mary stood outside crying, and then saw two angels when she looked inside the tomb. They asked her why she was crying, and she told them that they had taken away her Lord. She suddenly saw Jesus but did not recognise Him, thinking He was a gardener. She asked Him to tell her where He had put Him. Jesus called her name, "*Mary!*" Then she recognised Him and said, "*Rabboni*" (Teacher in Hebrew). Jesus told her not to hold Him because He had not yet ascended to His Father, but she should go and tell the disciples.

Jesus appeared that evening to the disciples and showed them His hands and side. He then breathed on them and put the Holy Spirit in them, saying that if they forgave the sins of anyone, they would be forgiven, but if they did not forgive them, their sins would be retained. Thomas, who was not with them, refused to believe they had seen Jesus, saying that unless he saw the wounds made by the crucifixion and personally touched Him, he would not believe them.

Jesus later appeared before them and told Thomas to touch His sides. He then castigated him for being faithless and said, "*Blessed are those who do not see and yet believe.*"

This book of John was written so that we may believe that Jesus is the Christ, the Son of God, and in believing that, we may have life through His Name.

After that, Jesus showed Himself again to the disciples by the Sea of Tiberias where they were all fishing but could not catch anything. Jesus shouted at them to put their nets on the other side of the boat, and they caught so many that they could not bring them in. They had not recognised Jesus at first, but on reaching land, they saw a charcoal fire, and Jesus told them to put some of the fish on the fire. They had caught a hundred and fifty-three large fish, but the net did not tear.

Jesus broke bread, and they had breakfast. He asked Simon Peter three times whether he loved Him. The first time Peter replied in the affirmative, Jesus said, "*Feed My lambs.*" The second time Jesus said, "*Tend My sheep,*" and the third time He said, "*Feed My sheep.*" He then told Peter that when he was young, he could do as he liked but when he grows old, he will hold out his hands, and someone will tease him and take him where he does not want to go. He said this to indicate by what kind of death he would glorify God.

Jesus then said, "*Follow Me,*" and Peter saw that John was following Him and was told to mind his own business when he complained. It was believed then by the disciples that John would not die.

There are many things that Jesus did, but there would not be enough room in the world to hold all the books if everything He did were written down.

THE ACTS OF THE APOSTLES

The traditional author of this book is Luke.

Jesus kept appearing to His disciples for forty days and discussing the Kingdom of God. He told them not to leave Jerusalem but to wait for what the Father had promised. They asked Him if He would restore the kingdom to Israel and He told them it was only God's business and that their time would come when they would receive the Holy Spirit. Jesus then disappeared into a cloud.

The disciples Peter, James, John, Andrew, Thomas, Bartholomew, Matthew, Philip, James (son of Alphaeus), Simon the Zealot, and Thaddaeus went with Mary Magdalene, Mary the mother of Jesus, and His brothers, back to Jerusalem.

Judas Iscariot, who had used the money he got for betraying Jesus to buy a field, fell down one day, burst his intestines, and died. The field was named *"Akeldama"* (the Field of Blood). The disciples later voted and picked Matthias to take Judas' place.

On the day of Pentecost, there was a roar and a huge wind with *"tongues like flames"* came from Heaven, and the disciples were filled with the Holy Spirit. They all started speaking in foreign languages though the crowd of Jews heard each one of them speak in his own language and could understand them. Peter told the crowd that the disciples were not drunk but what was happening had been prophesied by the prophet Joel (Joel 2: 28-32) that God would soon destroy the world and only those who called on His Name would be saved.

Peter told them that Jesus did many miraculous and good things, yet they still crucified Him. He was now sitting on the right hand of God. The people felt sorry and asked Peter what they should do; he told them to repent and be baptised in the Name of Jesus Christ in order for them to be forgiven and receive the gift of the Holy Spirit. The disciples baptised about three thousand people on that day. The believers sold all their property and gave the proceeds away and went to the Temple every day praising God and enjoying His goodwill.

Peter and John went up to the Temple one day, and they healed a lame man, making him walk by using Jesus' Name. The people were all amazed and praised God. They all surrounded Peter and the man who could now walk. Peter told them that they should not be surprised because it was this same Jesus whom they crucified who had performed that miracle through him. God knows that they did not know what they were doing, he said, and they should repent, and all their sins would be forgiven.

The Sadducees heard the disciples preaching and locked them up, but by then they had increased their followers to about five thousand. The next day, they were put in front of Caiaphas, Annas the high priest, and the other rulers. They were asked by what name and through what power they had healed the cripple. Peter, who was filled with the Holy Spirit, told them that everything was in the Name of Jesus Christ whom they had crucified.

They warned the disciples never to speak about Jesus again, but Peter refused, and they could do nothing to him because the crowd were many, all praising God. So they were all set free and went to pray to God. The meeting place shook, and they were all filled with the Holy Spirit. They were all one in heart and soul, even sharing their belongings together.

The followers sold their property and gave the money to the disciples, who were now called apostles. They distributed the money to the needy. One man called Ananias tried to cheat by selling his property but keeping some of the money for himself. Peter told him that he was only deceiving God. Ananias immediately fell down and died. He was quickly buried. His wife Sapphira, who knew of her husband's plan, was castigated by Peter, and she also fell down and died. She was buried beside her husband, and the whole church was in awe.

The people held the apostles in great esteem as they continued to do miraculous things. They carried all their sick to Peter who cured all of them. The chief priests jailed them, but an angel came into the jail and let them out, telling them to continue preaching to the people about the new life.

They were one day caught preaching in the Temple, and the soldiers brought them back in front of the chief priests who asked them why they continued to preach after being told not to. Peter told them that they only obeyed God and not men, and that Jesus was at the right hand of God who had raised Him up after they had crucified Him. God will always bestow the Holy Spirit on those who obey Him.

A Pharisee called Gamaliel told the priests privately to be careful what they did with the apostles because some time back a certain Theudas appeared, claiming to be somebody, and had acquired four hundred followers. He was killed, and his followers were dispersed. Another Galilean called Judas led an uprising but failed, so if what the apostles are doing is human, it will also fail on its own, but if it is really from God then no one can stop them.

So they flogged the apostles and let them go. They continued to preach Christ Jesus in the Temple and at home. The Word of God kept spreading, and the followers increased. Even some of the priests joined them. Some of the followers were allotted different tasks while the apostles continued teaching.

One of the chosen was called Stephen, who was full of faith and did notable wonders among the people. Some people were jealous and tried to instigate trouble against Stephen, saying they heard him speaking against God and blaspheming. They captured him and took him to the chief priests in the Sanhedrin (Tribunal), accusing him of saying that Jesus would come and destroy them.

When the priests asked him if these statements were true, Stephen related the history of their land from Abraham right down through Moses to the time Solomon built the Temple, saying that they had all sinned against the Holy Spirit, just like their fathers, and they had killed all the prophets who were working for God, including His Son Jesus Christ. They knew the Law, but they did not keep it.

When Stephen said he could see Heaven opening and Jesus sitting at the right hand of God, they were so angry they threw him outside and stoned him to death. On dying, Stephen asked God not to hold this sin against them.

Severe persecution broke out against the church in Jerusalem so that all except the apostles were dispersed throughout Judea and Samaria. Saul caused havoc with the church and imprisoned many people, but the Message continued to spread through the people who went to different towns.

Philip went to Samaria, preaching, baptising, and healing people. He even managed to disgrace a magician called Simon who people thought had power from God.

Peter and John went to Samaria on hearing of Philip's success and the converts received the Holy Spirit. Simon the magician tried to offer them money for them to give him the power of healing but was told to repent and God would forgive him.

They went back to Jerusalem preaching. Philip was told by an angel to go and meet a eunuch who was riding in a chariot on the road from Jerusalem to Gaza. He baptised the eunuch (an Ethiopian), after he confessed that he believed Jesus Christ was the Son of God. An angel then took Philip away, and he was found at Azotus.

Saul requested letters from the Damascus synagogues so that he could bring back as prisoners those who were of "the Way," or followers of Christ. On his way to Damascus a light from Heaven came, knocked him to the ground and blinded him. He then heard Jesus' voice asking him why he was persecuting them. He was afraid and asked Jesus what he should do. He was told to return to Damascus where he remained blind and could not eat or drink for three days. One of the converts, Ananias, was told by God in a vision to go to Saul and open his eyes. On regaining his sight, Saul was baptised and ate some food to regain his strength.

Saul started preaching Jesus in the synagogues, claiming Him to be the Son of God and those who knew him before as a persecutor were amazed. The Jews conspired to kill him, but his disciples took him in a basket at night and let him down over a wall. He went to Jerusalem and, after initial suspicion, was united with the apostles after Barnabas had explained that he was a changed man after seeing the Lord. Saul continued to preach, but the Jews wanted to murder him, so the apostles helped him to escape to Caesarea and then sent him off to Tarsus.

The church continued to increase in numbers as they enjoyed peace with encouragement from the Holy Spirit. Using Jesus' Name, Peter healed a paralytic called Aeneas who had been bedridden for eight years. The people of Lydda and Sharon saw this and turned to God.

At Joppa, a female disciple called Tabitha died but was brought back from the dead by Peter, and everybody praised God.

One day an angel appeared in a vision to Cornelius, a captain of the Italian cohort who was living in Caesarea. The angel told him to send some men to Joppa to look for Peter, who was staying with a man called Simon the tanner.

Meanwhile Peter was praying and felt hungry. God sent some animals and birds in a wide sheet and told him to eat because they had been purified by Him. This happened three times, and the thing was immediately taken up to Heaven.

The men sent by Cornelius came to Peter and took him to his house. On meeting Cornelius, Peter recounted all that Jesus went through up to the resurrection, saying that all who believe in Him will be forgiven through His Name. All who were listening were filled with the Holy Spirit, and Peter baptised them.

The Lord's Message spread as far as Phoenicia, Cyprus, and Antioch through those who were dispersed during the persecuting, which followed the stoning of Stephen. Barnabas was sent from Jerusalem to encourage them to remain loyal to God. He then went to Tarsus and brought Saul to Antioch where they continued teaching.

A prophet named Agabus prophesied a famine in the reign of Claudius, so the disciples sent a contribution to the brothers who lived in Judea through Barnabas and Saul.

King Herod started persecuting the church. He killed James (Zebedee), arrested Peter, and put him in prison. He wanted to hand him over to the people after Passover. An angel came, however, took Peter out of jail, and left him outside the city. He went to Mary's (mother of John) house and explained, to her astonishment, what the angel had done. He told her to go and tell the other disciples. Herod executed the guards when he heard that Peter had escaped to Caesarea. The Tyrians sued for peace with Herod, who was angry with them, but on the day of the ceremony, Herod was struck by an angel and died. He was eaten by worms. The Word of God kept on multiplying. Barnabas and Saul had gone to Jerusalem, and when they finished their ministry there, they returned to Antioch.

The Holy Spirit told the prophets and teachers of the Lord that He had some special work for Saul (now called Paul) and Barnabas. They travelled to Seleucia then on to Cyprus and Salamis, preaching the Word of God in the Jewish synagogues, helped by a follower called John. Paul then blinded a magician who had tried to turn the proconsul, whom they were converting, away from them. The proconsul immediately believed in God. This was in Paphos.

Paul and his company went to Perga in Pamphylia, where John left them and went back to Jerusalem. They then continued to Pisidian Antioch, where Paul started preaching, telling the people what God had done for the Israelites from the time He led them out of Egypt right up to the time of Jesus' crucifixion and resurrection. He explained that the people suffered because they did not do as God wished and committed many sins. Now he has brought them good news, and those who repent will be forgiven by God. Many were converted, and the Jews became jealous of the crowds. Paul told the Jews that God's Message was first spoken to them, but they rejected it, and that is why they were now teaching it to the Gentiles.

The Jews had Paul and Barnabas thrown out of the city, and they went to Iconium, where they were almost stoned because of instigation by the Jews, so they moved on to the Lycaonian towns of Lystra and Derbe.

At Lystra, Paul made a lame man walk because of his faith. The crowd were amazed and nicknamed Barnabas as Zeus and Paul as Hermes (the names of Greek gods). They then brought Paul and Barnabas sacrifices, but this made them angry. They told them they were human like them and had only come to spread the Message of God, who made Heaven and earth and gave them everything.

The Jews came from Antioch and persuaded the crowd to stone Paul. They dragged him out of the city, thinking he was dead. The disciples later helped him escape with Barnabas to Derbe. They continued preaching and appointed elders for them in each church who were committed to fasting, prayer, and belief in the Lord.

They then travelled to Pisidia, Pamphylia, Perga, and Attaliah, and finally back to Antioch where they told their followers all the good things God had done for them.

Paul and Barnabas returned to Jerusalem to find out from the apostles whether one needed to be circumcised in order to be saved, but Peter told the assembly that they could be saved only through the Grace of Jesus Christ. They should only abstain from anything contaminated by idols, from unchastity, and from the blood and meat of strangled animals.

Paul and Barnabas narrated their experiences to the assembly, who were so happy with what the two had achieved that they gave them more men to go with them back to Antioch. These included a man called Judas and Silas. John, who had left them in Pamphylia, wanted to go with them on a journey to visit all the towns in which they had taught to see how they were getting along. Paul did not want him to go, but Barnabas did, and they quarrelled so Barnabas took John (also called Mark) with him to Cyprus.

Paul went with Silas through Syria and Cilicia. Paul baptised Timothy at Lystra and took him along on his travels. The church grew stronger because of their teachings.

Paul had a vision from God to go to Macedonia, so he went to Philippi, the main city in Macedonia. They stayed at the house of a devout woman called Lydia. Paul took the evil spirit out of a fortuneteller who was making money for certain people. When her owners realised their means of profit had gone, they grabbed Paul and Silas, accused them of causing a disturbance, and took them in front of the authorities, who had them flogged and thrown into jail. An earthquake blasted the prison doors open, and the warden was converted by Paul. The authorities had to apologise to them and release them on learning that they were Romans and not Jews.

They then went to Thessalonica, where Paul explained to the Jews in the synagogue about Jesus Christ. The Jews got jealous and told the authorities that they were proclaiming another king to Caesar in the Name of Jesus. So Paul and his people left to Berea, where they had a lot of success until the Jews from Thessalonica came and stirred up trouble.

Paul left for Athens, leaving Silas and Timothy behind, with instructions to join him there later. Paul started preaching Jesus to the people and was grabbed and sent to their council (the Areopagus) in order to explain his teaching. Paul explained how God had made everything and so they should follow Him instead of idols. Before, man was ignorant, so God overlooked everything, but now the time had come to revere Him and obey Him because He has fixed a time that He will judge the world righteously through a Man whom He has destined for the task. He had already proved this by raising Him from the dead.

Paul left Athens for Corinth, having converted a few adherents. At Corinth, he stayed with Aquila and his wife, Priscilla, who had left Italy because of Claudius' order that all Jews must leave Rome. Silas and Timothy came from Macedonia. Paul got fed up with the Jews and said that he would only teach Gentiles. He moved on and stayed with a man called Titus Justus. He stayed for eighteen months, preaching the Word of God.

When Gallio was the Preconsul of Achaia, the Jews went against Paul and took him to court, but Gallio threw all of them out, saying it was not a criminal matter. So they got hold of Sosthenes, the ruler of the synagogue, and gave him a beating.

Paul then went to Syria with Aquila and Priscilla. From there, he went to Ephesus, preached for a few days, and then left them to go to Antioch. He continued to Phrygia, strengthening all his disciples.

A Jew called Apollos was converted by Priscilla and Aquila, who sent word to those in Achaia to welcome him when he arrived there. While Apollos was in Corinth, Paul went to Ephesus and baptised about twelve into the Name of the Lord Jesus Christ, and when he placed his hands on them the Holy Spirit came on them. He also taught in the synagogues for three months, but on encountering opposition from non-believers, he left them and taught daily in the school of Tyrannus for two years, converting the whole population. He also healed all the sick and cast out all the evil spirits.

Some Jews who practised exorcism tried to use Jesus' Name to expel the evil spirits from those who had them and failed. Everybody was in awe of Jesus. Many came to confess their magic practices and burn all their books about magic arts.

Paul sent Timothy and Erastus to Macedonia while he stayed in Asia. A silversmith called Demetrius, who made shrines of Artemis, caused confusion against Paul who was seen as a threat to his trade as people were no longer buying silver for their idols. The town clerk averted a riot by telling

Demetrius to solve his problems in court. Paul was advised to keep away until the tumult had died down.

He then left Macedonia, arriving in Greece where he spent three months. He and a few followers later went to Troas and spent a week. He raised a man called Eutychus from the dead after he had fallen from the third floor of a house.

They then sailed to Assos through several towns, preaching and telling several people to repent. Paul then bade farewell to his followers and went past Cyprus and on to Tyre to look for the disciples there, who advised him not to go to Jerusalem.

So Paul and his group went to Caesarea and met Philip the evangelist. He and a prophet called Agabus could not dissuade Paul from going to Jerusalem because he was prepared to die for Jesus Christ. They called on the elders, who advised him to undergo a purification ritual and shave his head so that the Jews would not believe the rumours that they had heard about him preaching against the Law of Moses.

He was, however, recognised and accused of defiling the holy place and bringing Greeks into the Temple. They tried to kill him but he was saved by some soldiers, chained, and taken to the barracks.

Paul then got permission to speak to the crowd. He told them he was a Jew and not an Egyptian or a Greek as they had thought. He also told them how he met Jesus, who asked him why he was persecuting him, in a vision; he explained how he became blind and regained his sight; and he said Ananias told him to repent and be saved. The crowd were not impressed, and he was saved by the soldiers who were about to flog him, but who had to let him go when he said he was a Roman.

They took him to face the chief priests in the Sanhedrin. Paul said he had behaved himself in the presence of God and his conscience was clear. Ananias the chief priest ordered his attendants to hit him in the mouth for insulting the "*high priest of God.*"

Paul then caused confusion between the Pharisees and the Sadducees by saying he was a Pharisee accused because he had hope in the resurrection of the dead, knowing that the Sadducees did not believe in resurrection. There was an argument, so Lysias, the commander of the soldiers, sent a detachment to snatch Paul back to the barracks in case he was killed.

About forty Jews conspired to kill Paul by tricking him out of the barracks to the Sanhedrin so that they would ambush him on the way, but he was warned by his nephew. Lysias got some troops and cavalry to escort Paul away to Caesarea where he was safely put in Herod's palace whilst awaiting his accusers.

Ananias came five days later to present the evidence against Paul to Governor Felix. He told him that Paul had stirred up trouble amongst the Jews and tried to defile the Temple, so they seized him, and he was saved by Lysias, the commander.

Paul told Felix that he had only been in Jerusalem for twelve days, and they could not produce any evidence to substantiate the charges. He said he believed in God and worshipped Him so his conscience was clear. Felix said he would decide the case after talking with Lysias.

Felix used to summon Paul to come and lecture him, hoping to get money out of him. This went on for two years until Felix was succeeded by Pontius Festus, and to curry favour with the Jews, Felix left Paul imprisoned.

Festus passed through Jerusalem on his way to Caesarea and was confronted by the priests, demanding that Paul be punished. At Caesarea, Festus called a tribunal to hear Paul's case. Paul said that he had done nothing wrong against Jewish law, the Temple, or Caesar. He was ready to die if he had indeed done something wrong. The charges brought by the priests were weighty but unsubstantiated, so Paul said he was ready to appeal to Caesar.

King Agrippa and Bernice (his sister and wife) arrived at Caesarea to see Festus, and they also heard Paul's case. He told Agrippa how he used to persecute the Jews with authority from the chief priests, and many were executed because of him. He then had a vision from God who told him what to do. He changed and started preaching, telling people to repent and turn to God. That is why he was seized by the Jews who wanted to kill him. All he has been saying is what Moses and the prophets said would happen. Agrippa said he found nothing wrong in what Paul had done, and he would have been set free if he had not appealed to Caesar.

Paul was put on a prison ship under the care of the captain Julius, and they sailed through several cities, almost drowning when they encountered a hurricane near Crete. They had to throw all their cargo and tackle overboard in order to be able to contain the storm. Paul calmed the crew, saying that he had heard from God that they would be safe. He took some bread and gave thanks to God. Soon after, they grounded the ship, and all 276 people on board swam safely to the shore of Malta.

The natives were friendly and gave them food. When a viper went on to Paul's hand without biting him, they all thought he was a god. Publius, the chief of the island, entertained them generously, and Paul cured his father of dysentery. After that, he cured everybody who was sick on the island.

After three months, they finally got a ship and arrived in Rome. The other prisoners were locked up except Paul, who had house arrest. Paul then told the Jews what had happened to him and why he was appealing to Caesar, but nobody had heard anything about him in Rome. Paul then told a large audience about Jesus and God's Word. Some believed, but some didn't after he had said that the Holy Spirit had spoken through Isaiah. Paul stayed for two years preaching the Kingdom of God without any hindrance.

PAUL's EPISTLE TO THE ROMANS

This is Paul's epistle (letter) to the Romans, telling them that he was chosen by God to do His Work on earth. "Whoever is righteous through faith will live. God has shown us what He likes and dislikes, so He will be angry with those who do evil things. We have no excuse because His works are there for all to see. We must always give thanks and praise Him, but people have not done that, and those who claimed to be wise, became foolish, worshipping idols and images. So God abandoned them, and men became homosexuals and did other unnatural things, therefore attracting punishment to themselves.

"Men have now become wicked, immoral, depraved, greedy, envious, murderous, quarrelsome, deceitful, malignant, proud, boastful, evil, and disobedient to parents; without conscience, faith, natural affection, or pity; insolent, gossipy, slanderous, and God haters. Man does evil things knowing very well that God does not like it. God will reward and punish each person according to his deeds. No one will escape. He rewards those who are good with eternal life and those who are evil with affliction, anxiety, indignation, fury, and death.

"God shows no favouritism. Those who sin without knowing the Law will be lost, and those who sin under the Law will be judged by the Law. What the Law requires is written in our hearts while our conscience bears witness and our thoughts accuse or defend one another. Those who preach God's Word should not in turn do evil. Circumcision is a matter of the heart and not a physical act, a spiritual observance rather than a mere observance of the Law. Any person who does this will be praised by God. Even if one is uncircumcised and obeys God's Word, it would be as if he was circumcised, and God will judge him rightly. Jews therefore, have no advantage over Gentiles. Nobody is perfect. We have all strayed and are sinners who don't revere God, but through the Grace of Jesus Christ who spilt His Blood for us, we can now be forgiven by God if we repent.

"Above all we must have faith in Jesus Christ because there is only one God who will judge us all by our faith, just like Abraham who was given righteousness by God because of his faith in Him. Sin came about through one man, and many have suffered as a result. In the same way, one righteous act can bring justification and life to all men. When Christ died, our sins died with Him and in the resurrection, He became new, just as those who follow Him will become clean. We must not succumb to sin but rather offer ourselves to God. What have we gained from our past sins? Nothing! Death is the consequence. But when we leave sin and turn to God, eternal life will be our reward. The wages of sin is death, but the gift of God is eternal life through Jesus Christ.

"Man is only bound by the Law in his lifetime, after that he is under a new obligation with the Spirit. In one's heart, one may agree with God's Law but in his own natural make up, one observes another law, battling against the principles which his reason dictates, and making him a prisoner to the law of sin that controls his actions. Because Jesus Christ came, His life-giving principles of the Spirit have freed us from the control of the principles of sin and death. Those under the control of the flesh cannot please God and will die, but those under the control of the Spirit will live in peace.

"Man must suffer while awaiting his bodily redemption. That is how we are saved, by hoping for what we do not see and waiting patiently for it. God makes all things work together for good. If God can give His own Son up to be killed on our behalf then He will also favour those who come to Him. God is the Acquitter, and Jesus is the One who died and now sits at God's right hand. Nothing can therefore separate us from the love of God that is in Christ Jesus. Everything works through God's mercy, which He shows to those whom He has chosen. One cannot contemplate what would happen if God was to show His anger and power against us."

Paul then quotes from the prophets, such as Hosea and Isaiah, in order to stress his point about God calling those who were formerly not with Him, into His fold. Righteousness is acquired through faith and not by works.

Paul continued by saying that his heart's desire and prayer to God is for everyone to have their salvation. "To obtain salvation, you have to submit to righteousness and the Will of God. If one confesses with his mouth the Lord Jesus Christ and truly believes in his heart that God raised Him from the dead, then he will be saved. The mouth confesses and the heart believes . . . that is the way to salvation.

"Not everyone has heard the good news about God. Faith results from hearing the Message of Christ, which is always near us and in our hearts. God is kind so we should remain in His kindness, otherwise we might be cut off from Him. God classes all men as disobedient so that He might have mercy on us all. He does not owe anybody anything. Everything is from Him, through Him, and to Him. The Glory is to Him forever.

"Nobody should think too highly of himself because God has measured out to each person his portion of faith. We have all been given certain gifts by God in order for us to form a cohesive whole in oneness with Him, so we should use whatever God has given us to the best of our ability.

"Let your love be sincere, cling to the good instead of the evil and always serve the Lord, joyfully hoping as you endure affliction. Be persistent in prayer and practise hospitality. Bless your persecutors and do not curse them. Share the joys of those who are happy and the grief of those who are sad.

"Live in harmony with others, do not aspire to eminence but associate yourself with humble people and do not be conceited. Do not pay back evil for evil. Do not avenge yourself but leave room for divine retribution. If your enemy is hungry or thirsty, feed him and overcome evil with good.

"Always obey the authorities because they were chosen by God, so to resist them means going against God, and you will be punished. Do right and you will earn God's approval. Pay your taxes and honour those to whom honour is due. Owe no one and love your neighbour. Obey the Commandments and clothe yourself in Jesus Christ. Do not feel contempt for anyone because of his beliefs because only God can and will judge him. Do everything with God in mind and always give Him thanks because, alive or dead, we belong to God.

"Don't criticise anyone, because we must all face God's tribunal and give account of ourselves. Nothing is unclean; something only becomes unclean to the one who considers it unclean.

"The Kingdom of God consists of righteousness, peace, and joy in the Holy Spirit. Whoever serves Christ in this way is pleasing to God and is approved by men. Everything we do should contribute to one another's peace and development. Every act that does not spring from faith is a sin. Accept one another just as Christ accepts us for the glory of God. Keep an eye on those who cause divisions and temptations that are against what you have been taught and keep away from them because they do not serve God."

Paul ends the letter by sending greetings to all those who have helped him.

THE FIRST EPISTLE OF PAUL TO THE CORINTHIANS

This epistle was written by Paul in Ephesus on his third missionary journey. Paul, his friend Sosthenes, and his main followers were called to the church at Corinth. He wrote thanking God for giving them divine grace through Jesus Christ, so that on the day of judgement, they would not be blamed. He asked them to refrain from fighting and be united in mind and attitude towards Jesus because He died for them.

"The Message of the cross is God's power to those who are being saved. God helps the weak, foolish, despised, insignificant, and nobodies, in order to shame those who think they know it all, so that nobody may boast in God's presence. If one must boast, he must boast in the Lord. I am preaching the Message of Jesus Christ so that your faith might not rest on human wisdom but on divine strength. No eye has seen, no ear has heard, neither has the human heart thought of what God has prepared for those who love Him.

"God reveals everything to us through the Spirit, and a spiritual person judges the value of everything while he himself is valued by none. We can only know what God thinks through the mind of Christ. Everybody has been given a task by God. One does the planting, another does the watering, but it is God who causes the growth. He deserves credit and thanks for EVERYTHING. The planter and the waterer will, however, receive their just reward according to what they contributed. Like a building, Jesus Christ is the foundation for us to build on. Each one of us is God's Temple and His Spirit lives in all of us. If anyone destroys God's Temple, God will destroy him.

"One must become foolish in order to grow wise, for the wisdom of the world is folly in God's estimation. Don't

judge or criticise because nobody has given you that supe-
riority. The Kingdom of God is not a matter of words but of
power.

"Those who are incestuous should be handed over to
Satan for their flesh to be destroyed so that their spirits can
be saved on the day of the Lord Jesus Christ. Do not boast
or associate with sexually immoral people or with those
who are avaricious, grasping, idolatrous, abusive, robbers,
or drinkers. All those including the profligate, adulterers,
thieves, and homosexuals will not inherit the Kingdom of
God.

"The body is not for lust but for the Lord and the Lord
for the body. He who unites with a prostitute in sex becomes
one with her, and the two will become one flesh. But he who
unites with the Lord is one Spirit with Him. Sexual immorality is a sin against your own body and your body is a temple
of the Holy Spirit within you, which God gave to you, so that
means we do not belong to ourselves.

"Every man must have his own wife and every woman
her own husband. The husband has authority over his wife's
body, and the wife has authority over her husband's body.
They must not deprive each other except when they want
to devote themselves to prayer, otherwise Satan will tempt
them because of their lack of self-control. It is better to
marry than to be consumed with passion. There must be no
divorce, or your children will be unholy. Everybody has his
calling, so we do not know what we can do for one another
in marriage. Circumcision does not mean anything, only the
observance of God's Commandment counts. We must all accept our lot in life because we do not know what God has
got planned for us. Married people have divided interests
and cannot concentrate everything on the Lord, but it is,
however, no sin to marry. God understands everything. If a
woman's husband dies, she can remarry, but she is better off
remaining single.

"Not everyone knows that there is only one God, that is
why there is idolatry, but don't let your freedom of choice

hinder you from worshipping anything else other than the One and only God. Those who preach the good news shall live by the good news. In the past God has struck down those He was not pleased with as an example for us not to lust after evil or worship idols.

"In times of temptation, God will always provide a way out for those who are faithful to Him, because he is always faithful. God allows us to do everything, but not everything we do is helpful or constructive to us so we should be careful and do only those things that will make God happy.

"Do not eat any food that has already been offered to idols. Whatever you eat, drink or do, do it all to the glory of God. A man should not wear anything on his head while praying, and a woman should always cover her head or wear a veil while praying. A man should not cover his head because he is the image of God. Woman came from man, so he must have authority over her, but they both have their origin from God; therefore, they must show each other respect.

"Whoever eats and drinks without due appreciation of the Body of Christ, eats and drinks to his own condemnation. That is why many are weak, sick, and die. The Spirit distributes gifts of knowledge, wisdom, and power to whom He sees fit. We are all baptised into one body through Christ. God made the body in such a way that all parts are equal and have a purpose. If one part is missing or injured, the whole body will be affected.

"However, all one's gifts, faith, and powers are useless if one does not have love. Love is not selfish, jealous, out for display, conceited, unmannerly, self-seeking, irritable, prejudiced, does not bear a grudge, and takes no pleasure in injustice but sides happily with the truth. Out of the three, faith, hope, and love, the greatest is love, because it never fails.

"He who speaks in tongues is speaking to God because no one else can understand him. He who prophesies is more important, however, because he gives people a constructive, encouraging, and comforting message. Women should keep silent in churches because they are not allowed to speak.

They must be in subordination. If they wish to learn something, they must ask their husbands at home. It is improper for a woman to speak in church."

Paul continues, "I am the last of the apostles who Christ appeared to, even though I don't deserve to be called one because I once persecuted the Church of God. I have worked hard with God to spread His Message.

"Christ died for us and was raised from the dead, so those who say there is no resurrection are wrong. Christ died in order that we might live and that our sins might be cleansed. The end will come when Christ hands over His Kingdom back to God and all His enemies will be under His feet. Flesh and blood cannot inherit the Kingdom of God, only the spirit can do that."

Paul ends the letter by saying that he would remain in Ephesus, but Timothy and Apollos would visit them so they should try and treat them well. He tells them to be alert, stand firm in faith, be strong, do everything in love, and the Grace of the Lord Jesus be with them.

THE SECOND EPISTLE OF PAUL TO THE CORINTHIANS

This was written by Paul in Macedonia on his third mission-ary journey, as a result of a report brought to him by Titus concerning the church.

"God rescued us from death and will always rescue us be-cause we look up to Him for deliverance. God is trustworthy, and anything that Jesus promises will be fulfilled by God.

"There is liberty where the Spirit of the Lord is. We do not proclaim ourselves but Jesus Christ as Lord and ourselves as servants for His sake, because God has made the light shine in our hearts so as to show the knowledge of His glory in the face of Christ. Because we believe in Jesus, our inner self is renewed day after day even though our outer nature suffers decay. Visible things are transitory, but the unseen things are everlasting.

"We know that we have a place to go when we leave our earthly bodies, so God has granted us the Spirit to keep us confident, knowing that being at home in the body means being absent from the Lord, for we walk by faith and not by sight.

"We must try to please God because we will all have to appear before the judgement seat of Christ so that we may receive as our due what we practised while in our body, whether good or bad. That is why we have tried to win people over to God because everything we do and teach is with the aim of pleasing Him. God sent Christ to die for us in order to reconcile the world. We must cleanse ourselves from every defilement of the flesh and spirit and complete our dedica-tion in reverence of God.

"I know my last letter made you sad, but I am glad because your grief led to repentance, and that is what God wanted, so that He could save you. I'm sending Titus to you because his zeal has been tested, and he has so much confidence in you. Show him and the others with him proof of your love. If you sow liberally, you will reap liberally. God loves a happy giver, and He is able to give you every possible Grace so that you will never be in need. His righteousness never fails.

"I belong to Christ as much as you, even though I have been given the authority to boast and talk about it. I feel I belong to Christ because of what I've been through: floggings, facing death, lashings, beatings, shipwrecked, and in danger from robbers and false brothers. I have been weary from sleepless nights, hunger, and thirst, and I have been let down out of a window in a basket to escape the governor in Damascus. Even though I boast, I do it in Christ's Name and not about myself. I am happy with my weaknesses and sufferings because they are on account of Christ. When I am weak is when I am strong.

"I am writing all this so that when I arrive I will be happy with you. I am afraid though that some of you may have reverted back to your old ways of strife, jealousy, ugly temper, sectarianism slander, gossip, conceit, and disharmony and that God will humble me in front of you for having failed you.

"This will be my third visit to you, and I will not spare those who have sinned since you are looking for proof of Christ's speaking through me. Examine yourselves, whether you have enough faith to pass the test. Pray to God that you may do no wrong. Mind your ways, accept admonition, preserve peace, and the God of love and peace will be with you."

THE EPISTLE OF PAUL TO THE GALATIANS

This is a short but important letter by Paul, containing a protest against legalism and a clear statement of the gospel of God's grace. It was written shortly after the close of the first missionary journey to the churches of Galatia.

"I am disturbed that you are so readily turning away from God's gospel. If anyone else teaches you anything that differs from what we have preached to you, a curse on him. What is preached by me came from a revelation of Jesus Christ and not from a human being."

Paul then explains how he used to persecute the church until his revelation and how he did not come into contact with any apostles as he went on his travels. It was fourteen years later before he went to Jerusalem with the good news. The power that made Peter an apostle to the circumcised (the Jews) was the same power that made him (Paul) an apostle to the uncircumcised (the Gentiles). He even reprimanded Peter and the other apostles for deviating from God's path.

He says, "If you Galatians do not live like Christ, then it means He died for nothing. Those who depend on the works of the law live under a curse. One must live by faith.

"God gave His Law to Abraham, and you are supposed to follow the Laws of God. The Laws were given to show sin in its true light, so that we might know right from wrong. Through our faith in Jesus Christ, we should automatically follow God's Law. You should never have to go back to the other so-called gods now that you know God and He knows you. So how come you are reverting back to your old ways? Did I do all my teaching of you for nothing? What made you change? You must be guided by the Spirit and not the flesh, for those who live by the flesh will not inherit God's Kingdom.

"Carry one another's burden, and if someone does wrong, set him straight in a humble spirit because nobody is perfect. Love one another and fulfil the Law of Christ. God will not be mocked. What a person sows is what he will reap. The one who sows for his own flesh will harvest rain from his flesh, while the one who sows for the Spirit will harvest eternal life from the Spirit. Practise only what is right and beneficial to everyone. The Grace of our Lord Jesus Christ be with your spirit. Amen."

THE EPISTLE OF PAUL TO THE EPHESIANS

This was written by Paul while a prisoner, most likely in Rome, to a number of churches including Ephesus.

"Blessed be God for giving us Jesus Christ in whom we enjoy redemption, the forgiveness of our sins, and the wealth of His Grace, which He poured out on us through His Blood. When I hear about your faith in Jesus Christ and your love of all saints, I never fail to give thanks for you in my prayers, that God might grant you wisdom and revelation to understand Him.

"God is rich in mercy. That is why He gave us Jesus Christ, so that our sins might be forgiven. For we are saved by Grace through faith and not by who we are; it is God's gift. It is not by works, so no one can boast. We are His handiwork, created in Jesus for good works so that we should live in them.

"Jesus united Jews and Gentiles and brought the hostility to an end by dying on the cross. We are all members of God's household, of which Christ is the cornerstone.

"God's grace was bestowed on me to teach the secrets of Christ, which had up till now been hidden with God. So I advise you all to conduct yourselves in a manner worthy of the calling you have received with humility, gentleness, patience, and love, making every effort to preserve the unity of the Spirit in the bond of peace.

"Do not behave like the Gentiles whose lives are spent in the uselessness of their ways of thinking and because of the obstinacy of their hearts, have grown estranged from the Divine Life. You must rid yourselves of your previous habits, which are corrupted by deceitful lusts, and renew yourselves with a nature that is created in God's Likeness in genuine righteousness and holiness.

"Always speak the truth to each other and commit no sin when you are angry, so as not to give the devil an opportunity. Do not steal and allow foul speech to come out of your mouth. Never cause the Holy Spirit any grief. Get rid of all bitterness, bad temper, clamour, abusive language, and all malice. Be kind, tender hearted, and forgiving to one another, just as God has in Christ forgiven you and loved you.

"None of you should be guilty of greed, immorality, idolatry, falsehoods, debauchery, drunkenness, and any kind of evil, otherwise God will not be pleased. Wives should submit to their husbands as the head of the household just as Christ is the Head of the Church. Husbands must love their wives as their own bodies. Children should be obedient and honour their parents. Slaves should obey their masters but render service to the Lord and not to men.

"Whatever good one does will be recompensed by God. Masters must treat their slaves in the same way. Be strong in the Lord so that you will be able to stand against the devil's intrigues. For we are not fighting against flesh and blood opponents but against the rulers, the authorities, the cosmic powers of this present darkness, and against the spiritual forces of evil in the heavenly spheres.

"I have sent you Tychicus to give you all the information about us and encourage you. Peace, love, and faith from God and Jesus."

THE EPISTLE OF PAUL TO THE PHILIPPIANS

This is the letter written by Paul in prison, most likely in Rome to thank the church for the gift of money sent him through Epaphroditus. Epaphroditus subsequently became seriously ill and was nursed back to health by Paul, who now sends him back to Philippi with this letter. The main emphasis is of joy and triumphant faith.

"Every time I think of you, I thank my God and pray for all of you with joyfulness for your fellowship in furthering the good news. I pray that your love may grow ever richer in real knowledge and all judgement and that you may be unsullied and blameless as you face the day of Christ.

"You should know that my imprisonment is because I belong to Christ, and the brothers in the Lord have been encouraged to be far more daring in spreading the Divine Message without fear. Conduct yourselves in a manner worthy of the good news concerning Christ so that whether I come and see you, or I am absent, I may hear that you are standing firm in one spirit and one mind.

"Know that Christ suffered and humbled himself for you, and God lifted Him high so that at the Name of Jesus, every knee shall bow in Heaven and Earth and every tongue should confess that Jesus is the Lord to the Glory of God.

"I hope to send you Timothy shortly so that I too may be cheered by news from you. I am sending you my brother Epaphroditus, who was ill but was saved by God. Therefore, welcome him with all joyfulness in the Lord. Be glad in the Lord and watch out for those wicked workers and those who confide in the flesh and not in Jesus. Always pray to God and thank Him. So will the Peace of God, which surpasses all understanding, keep guard over your hearts and your thoughts in Jesus Christ. Put your mind only on whatever is righteous and may the God of peace be with you.

"I am grateful to you Philippians because you have always supported me with gifts and even went into partnership with me with regard to giving and receiving. I have received what you sent through Epaphroditus, and now I have more than enough. God will fully supply all your needs. Greet every saint in Christ Jesus, and may the Grace of the Lord Jesus Christ be with your spirit."

THE EPISTLE OF PAUL TO THE COLOSSIANS

This was also written by Paul in prison, most likely in Rome when he was under house arrest. It was written to combat a serious Judaic-Gnostic error.

"We give thanks to God for we have heard of your faith in Jesus Christ and the love you cherish for all the saints, through the Spirit. We have prayed that all of you be filled with spiritual wisdom in order to do the right things and live in a way worthy of the Lord. All things in Heaven and on Earth were created through God. He holds everything together. Through Jesus' death, He has introduced us into His holy, blameless, and irreproachable presence. God chose me to preach His Word and the secrets that had been hidden for a long time, but have now been revealed through the saints. Even though I am physically absent, I am with you in spirit.

"Beware of those preaching deceit and falsehoods. Apply your mind to things above because your lives are now with Christ. God will be angry with disobedient people who are immoral, impure, evil, greedy, and worship idols.

"You used to do bad things before; now, however, you must stop that and work for God. Love each other, forgive each other, and clothe yourselves with tenderness of heart in order to enjoy God's love. Do everything in the Name of the Lord. Wives should be submissive to their husbands, and husbands should love their wives. Children should obey their parents, slaves should obey their masters, and masters should respect their slaves and treat them well. Treat outsiders well.

"Tychicus will tell you all about my affairs. All my brothers here send you their greetings. Extend our greetings to the brothers in Laodicea and to the church that meets in Nympha's home. Grace be with you."

THE FIRST EPISTLE OF PAUL TO THE THESSALONIANS

This was written by Paul during his second missionary journey, not long after he had founded the church. It is the first epistle written to encourage the Thessalonians' growth as Christians and to settle a question that was troubling them: whether those of their number who had died would miss some of the blessings of the second Coming of Christ.

"Grace to you and peace in God and Jesus. We pray for you often knowing the good works you have done and your transformation from serving idols to serving God.

"After suffering in Philippi, we took great courage with God's help to spread our message to you. We did this not to ingratiate ourselves but to please God. We thank God that you took our message in good faith, as you have now become true followers of Christ, having suffered in the hands of your countrymen for your belief. So we sent Timothy to encourage you in your faith, and he has returned with good news concerning your faith and love.

"We can never thank God enough for all the happiness He has given us. Continue living in the way you learnt from us, a way that is pleasing to God. Keep away from sexual immorality and take your wives in purity and honour. Don't take advantage of anybody, or God will punish you. Love one another, live in peace, and remember that Jesus died for you.

"On Judgement Day, those who died in Christ will rise first. Don't repay evil with evil, be helpful to each other, and always thank God for everything. Please read this letter to all the brothers, and the Grace of our Lord Jesus Christ be with you."

THE SECOND EPISTLE OF PAUL TO THE THESSALONIANS

This was written by Paul to correct some misconceptions concerning the second Coming of Christ.

"Grace to you and peace from God the Father and the Lord Jesus Christ. Your faith is growing so splendidly that we are always bound to give God thanks for you. Your love for one another is increasing, which is evidence of God's righteous judgement that you may be made worthy of His Kingdom. Those who ignore God will suffer everlasting ruin separated from His Presence and His Power. We constantly pray for you that God may render you worthy of His Call.

"Don't be deceived by false messages or letters allegedly sent by us to sway you from God's Cause. The apostasy will come first, and all sinners will be doomed. The coming of the lawless man is the work of Satan, and it will be accompanied by great power, signs, and miracles, all of them false. Those who do not follow God and are tempted by these false signs will be destroyed.

"So stand firm and hold on to the traditions you learned from us, and God will encourage and strengthen you in every good work and word. Avoid those who refuse to do the right things. Always set the right example for others to follow. Work hard to earn your own living, for those who are idle will not eat. Love each other, do good, and the Grace of the Lord Jesus Christ be with all of you."

THE FIRST EPISTLE OF PAUL
TO TIMOTHY

Timothy 1, Timothy 2, and Titus are also known as the Pastoral Epistles, which were written by Paul to his special envoys sent on specific missions in accordance with the needs of the hour. Timothy 1 was written to Timothy at Ephesus while Paul was still travelling in the coastal regions of the Aegean Sea.

"Grace, mercy and peace from God and Christ Jesus. Stay in Ephesus to warn certain people not to teach any other doctrine, and don't pay any attention to legends and interminable genealogies that cause disputes. The purpose of our instruction is love that rises out of a pure heart, a clear conscience, and undisguised faith.

"The Law is admirable if one makes lawful use of it, because it was not laid down for honest persons but for sinners. I am grateful to Christ Jesus, who strengthened me and considered me faithful enough to appoint me for service even though I was formerly a slanderer, persecutor, and insulter. But I found mercy so that in me, the foremost of sinners, Jesus Christ might display His unlimited patience, that I might be an example to all who would put their trust in Him for eternal life.

"Petitions, prayers, intercessions, and thanksgivings should be made for everybody. This is good and acceptable to God who wants all persons to be saved and know the truth. There is one God and one mediator between God and men, that man is Jesus Christ.

"Men everywhere should pray, and women who revere God should dress modestly without gold, pearls, or expensive clothes. Women should learn quietly with complete submission. They should not teach or domineer over men; instead, they should keep still.

"Whoever aspires to be a bishop must be above reproach, with only one wife, presiding well over his children and home. He must also enjoy a favourable reputation among the outsiders so that he may not fall into disgrace and into Satan's trap. The same attributes should apply to the deacons.

"The Spirit says that in later times some people will fall away from the faith and yield to deluding spirits and demonic teachings by hypocritical liars. Everything God created is good, and nothing should be rejected, but should be gratefully received. Train yourself for Godliness, for it holds promise for the present and the future. Devote yourself to public reading, preaching, and teaching. Treat older men as your fathers, younger men as your brothers, older women as your mothers, and younger women as your sisters with absolute purity. Whoever does not provide for his dependents and especially for his own family has denied the faith and is worse than a non-believer.

"Don't enrol a widow unless she is over sixty years of age, was the wife of one husband, and has a reputation for good works. Don't enrol younger widows who still have sensuous impulses. Don't recognise a charge against an elder unless it is supported by two or three witnesses. Observe these Commandments without discrimination or favouritism.

"Let all slaves show respect to their masters and vice versa. Piety and contentment is a great gain for we brought nothing into the world, and we can carry nothing out. The love of money is the root of all evils, and those who are eager to be rich fall into temptation and a snare and some have wandered away from the faith in a desire to have money. As a man of God, you should fight the good fight of faith. Shun money and all evil and instead go after righteousness, godliness, faith, love, patience, and gentleness in order to take hold of eternal life.

"Keep the Commandment stainless and irreproachable until the appearance of our Lord Jesus Christ, which will be made known in due course. Put all your hopes in God and command the rich not to be haughty and put their hope in the uncertainty of wealth. Lay a sound foundation for the future so that your people may take hold of the real life given by God. Grace be with you all."

THE SECOND EPISTLE OF PAUL TO TIMOTHY

This was written by Paul from Rome towards the end of the second imprisonment. The epistles concern church organisation and discipline, including such matters as the appointment of bishops and deacons, the opposition of heretical or rebellious members, and the provision for the maintenance of doctrinal purity.

"Grace, mercy and peace from God the Father and Christ Jesus our Lord. I am grateful to God whom I worship with a clear conscience, and I constantly remember you night and day in my prayers. Keep alive the flame of God's gracious gift that is in you, because He has given us a spirit of power, love, and self-control.

"He has appointed me a preacher, an apostle, and a teacher, and though I am suffering in this way, I believe He will look after me and keep me safe. All those in the province of Asia have deserted me, but may the Lord grant favour to Onesiphorous who often refreshed me even though I was a prisoner.

"Teach reliable men who will be able to teach others as well. God will grant you understanding in everything, so keep in mind Christ as you teach the good Word. If you deny Him, He will deny you. Do your best to be approved by God and keep away from the Godless and empty discussions. God's foundation stands firm. The Lord knows those who are His. Let everyone who names the Lord's Name stand aloof from wickedness.

"Keep away from the lusts of youth; go instead in pursuit of integrity, faith, love, and peace in fellowship with those who call on the Lord out of pure hearts. You must not quarrel but be kind to everyone, skilled in teaching, and willing to suffer wrong. You must correct in a gentle way those who go against God, in the hope that God may grant them repentance that leads to the acknowledgement of truth so that they may come to their senses and escape from the devil.

"In the last days, difficult times will come because people will be sinners who love pleasure more than God. Such people are those who captivate idle women and stop them ever trying to learn the knowledge of truth. They will not go far because their folly is obvious to everyone. But you have adhered to my teaching despite all the suffering that I've been put through.

"All who want to live devotedly in Christ will be persecuted. You must, however, remain faithful in what you have learnt. From childhood you have known the Holy Scriptures, which are able to make you wise for salvation through faith in Christ Jesus. All scripture is inspired by God and is profitable for teaching.

"Teach the Message with complete patience. A time will come when people will be more interested in hearing myths instead of the Scriptures but keep your head, endure hardship, and discharge your full duties as a minister. My time is coming soon. I have finished the race, fought the good fight, and kept my faith. God will award me and others like me the crown of righteousness.

"Visit me soon with Mark because I am alone with Luke. Even though everybody deserted me in my first defence, the Lord stood by me and strengthened me so that through me, the Message might be fully proclaimed and all the Gentiles might hear it. The Lord will rescue me from all evil acts and save me for His Heavenly Kingdom. The Lord be with your spirit. Grace be with you all."

THE EPISTLE OF PAUL TO TITUS

This epistle was written by Paul to Titus in Crete. "Grace and peace from God the Father and Christ Jesus our Saviour. I left you in Crete so that you might correct the defects and appoint elders to each town.

"A bishop must be irreproachable, not self-willed, hot tempered, a drunkard, pugnacious, or greedy for dishonest gain. He must be able to encourage people by his wholesome teaching and refute those who raise objections. These must be silenced before they can upset people, because their conscience is polluted, and they profess to know God but deny Him by their practices.

"The elder women should be sensible, chaste, good housekeepers, good natured, and submissive to their husbands so that they don't slander the Word of God. Urge the younger men as well to behave prudently. Slaves should be submissive to their masters, and masters should treat slaves with respect. Be subject to the ruling authorities and be obedient. Don't slander anyone, be gentle, and work hard. God has shown you His goodness, so you must also show love to Him and your fellow men. May Grace be with you all."

THE EPISTLE OF PAUL
TO PHILEMON

This was written by Paul during his first imprisonment in Rome. It deals with Philemon's runaway slave, Onesimus, who was converted through Paul, established in faith by him, and then sent back to Philemon with a plea that he (Onesimus) be forgiven for the wrong done to his master. The slave had apparently absconded with some of his master's money, which he had squandered, and Paul suggests that Philemon not insist on getting his money back and that Onesimus would repay it.

"I always give thanks to my God when I mention you in my prayers. I am sending Onesimus back to you so that you might take him back as a brother rather than a slave. Be good to him and I will be responsible for any debt he might owe you. Don't forget that over and above, you owe me your very self, and I would like to make some profit out of you in the Lord. The Grace of the Lord Jesus Christ be with your spirit."

THE EPISTLE OF PAUL
TO THE HEBREWS

This epistle is attributed to Paul, though the authorship is uncertain.

"God spoke to our fathers in the old days through the prophets and later on through Christ, who sustains the universe by His almighty Word. He became greater than all the angels, that is why He sits on the right hand of God. We must therefore listen and do all that He has said. How shall we escape if we neglect so great a salvation? He died so that He might destroy sin and death, which are the tools of the devil, and set free those who throughout life are held in slavery by fear of death.

"Every house is built by someone, but the Builder of all things is God, and Jesus is His Son and so is entitled to greater honour than even Moses.

"Give daily warnings to each other so that no one may fall away from the living God by not believing in Him and behaving wickedly. We have had the good news preached to us, unlike in the past when the Message heard by the people from the prophets did not sink in because it was not united by faith.

"Those who disobey God will not enter into His Kingdom. God does not forget any good or love that you show for His Name. He does not lie, and He has sworn that those who take refuge in Him will be given strong encouragement to live in His ways.

"The Lord has said that He will make a strong covenant with the Houses of Israel and Judah because they did not remain faithful to the old one. This time He says He will write His Laws in their hearts so that they don't forget, and He will be more merciful and not remember their sins.

"The old covenant consisted of food and drink offerings, with ablutions, various sacrifices, and physical regulations;

but with the Coming of Christ, things changed because He came only with the Holy Spirit and offered Himself as a flawless sacrifice to God. He is the mediator of the new Covenant that has been ratified by His Blood. There is no forgiveness without blood shedding. He has put away sin by sacrificing Himself. The blood of bulls and goats cannot take away sin.

"When Jesus said, '*Here I come to do Your Will*' (Psalm 40:6-8), He takes away the first covenant in order to establish the second. With a single offering of Himself, He has perfected those who are being made holy (like the priests). The greatest Priest of all, Jesus, is in charge of God's house, so we should be honest in our hearts and draw near to Him because He is faithful to us.

"We should be helpful and show love to each other. If we go on sinning wilfully after acquiring the knowledge of the truth, there will no longer be any sacrifice left for our sins, and a fierce fire will destroy those who oppose God. Don't throw away your confidence because it carries a rich reward. One needs endurance to gain the promised blessing upon accomplishing what God wants. On the Day of Judgement, only the righteous through faith will live. God will not be pleased with those who shrink back.

"Faith is an assurance of what is hoped for, a conviction of unseen realities. By faith we understand that the universe was created at God's command so that what we now see was made out of what cannot be seen. Without faith, it is impossible to please Him. He who comes to God must believe that He exists and that He is a rewarder of those who search for Him. Abel, Enoch, Noah, Abraham, Isaac, Jacob, Sarah, Moses, Gideon, Samson, David, Samuel, and the prophets all had faith when they died. Even Rahab, the harlot who saved two of Joshua's men from the King of Jericho, had faith when she received the spies and hid them in her house (Joshua 2). It was faith that made Abraham bring Isaac as an offering when he was tested. (Genesis 22).

"Faith has overcome kingdoms, administered justice, procured promised blessings, shut the mouth of lions, quenched the power of fire, escaped being killed by the sword, made powerful those who had been weak, became mighty in war, and turned foreign armies to flight.

"Women have received back their dead by resurrection. Others have suffered torture, mocking, flogging, chains, and imprisonment. All of these, while winning Divine approval through their faith, did not receive the promised blessing, for God had in view something better for us so that without us they would not be made perfect.

"Let us throw away our sins and follow Jesus, who is the cause and the completer of our faith and who died for us on a cross and is now seated on the right hand of God.

"Do not think lightly of the Lord's discipline and don't be discouraged under His reproof, for God disciplines the person He loves and punishes every son whom He receives. You must endure for the sake of correction, because God is only treating you as His son. He does it for our benefit so that we may share in His Holiness. Be at peace with everybody, don't be immoral, and don't be bitter about life.

"Be grateful that the Kingdom we have received cannot be shaken and let us serve God with reverence and awe. Show brotherly love and hospitality and keep in mind those who are in prison as if you are in prison with them, and the ill-treated as though you are suffering physically yourselves.

"Let marriage be held in honour and the marriage bed unpolluted, for God will judge the immoral and the adulterous. Let your conduct be free from the love of money and be satisfied with what you have because God will never desert you. Don't be led astray by strange teachings and let your heart be strengthened by grace and faith in Jesus Christ. Do not forget to do good and be generous, for such sacrifices make God happy. Obey your leaders and yield to them, because it is God who chose them to watch over your souls as persons who must give account. Timothy has been freed, and if he comes here soon, I will see you. Extend our greetings to all your leaders and to all the saints. Grace be with you all."

THE GENERAL EPISTLE
OF JAMES

This book was written by James to the Jewish Christians, to comfort them in their trials and to warn and rebuke them regarding the errors and the sins into which they had fallen.

"Consider it a complete joy when you become involved in all sorts of trials, well aware that testing of your faith brings out steadfastness. If you lack wisdom, ask God and it will be granted without reserve or reproach. But you should ask in faith without any doubt. Everyone should be happy with his position, because rich or poor, we will all die one day.

"Anyone who stands up under trial and passes the test will receive the crown of life God has promised to those who love Him. God cannot be tempted by evil, and He tempts no one. A person is tempted when he is drawn away and enticed by his own desire, which becomes sin and which produces death when it becomes too bad. Every beneficent gift and every perfect present is from God.

"Be quick to listen, slow to talk, and slow to get angry because anger does not promote God's righteousness. Be humble because in humility one receives the implanted word that is able to save souls. If one hears the Message, one must act on it. God has chosen the poor to be rich in faith and to be heirs of the Kingdom, which He has promised to those who love Him, so don't discriminate against anyone, because it is a sin.

"If you break one Commandment, it is as if you have broken them all, and you will be judged accordingly. The judgement is merciless to those who have shown no mercy. Faith must be joined with action because it is no good if you don't act on it.

"The tongue is used to praise God yet the same tongue is used to curse people. This is wrong so you should watch what you say. Don't cherish jealousy, rivalry, and lies in your heart. Friendship with the world is enmity towards God. You cannot love both. God opposes the haughty, but grants grace to the humble, therefore submit yourself to God, resist the devil, and he will flee from you. Draw near to God and He will draw near to you. Be humble and He will exalt you. Don't judge, insult, or criticise anyone because only God who has the power over life and death can do that.

"No one knows tomorrow, so one should always bear God in mind when making future plans. Life is a vapour that appears for a little while and disappears. He who knows what is right and fails to do it, commits a sin. Be strong and wait patiently for the Coming of the Lord. Job is a good example of how God is compassionate and merciful. Don't swear by heaven or earth or anything else, don't complain about one another, and let your yes be yes and your no be no.

"If you are suffering, you should pray or let the elders of the church pray for you, and if you are happy, you should sing psalms. By faith, your sins will be forgiven and all your illnesses cured. Confess your sins to each other and pray for one another. He who turns a sinner back from his evil ways will save his soul from death and will cover a great number of sins."

THE FIRST GENERAL EPISTLE OF PETER

This epistle was written by Peter the apostle, to encourage Christians who had been undergoing persecution. "I know you are a little distressed by your various trials. This is to prove your faith in Jesus who you do not see now, but the salvation of your souls will be the reward for your faith. Put your hopes on the grace that will be coming to you when Jesus is revealed, because you have been saved by His Blood. Love one another from the heart because you have been born again, which means you should lay aside all malice, deceit, pretence, envy, and slander, and be thirsty for spiritual milk like a new born baby.

"You are His chosen people who have been saved, so you should conduct yourselves well amongst the Gentiles so that even though they call you criminals, they will see your good works and glorify God. It's God's Will that you should be submissive towards authority. Enjoy liberty as slaves of God and treat everyone honourably.

"You domestic slaves should respect your masters. Bear patiently with your suffering when you are doing right and God will be pleased. Christ suffered for you and left behind an example for you to follow. He carried our sins in His own Body on a cross, and we are healed by His wounds.

"Wives should be submissive to their husbands and not be ostentatious, but respectful and chaste. In the same way, husbands should be understanding to their wives because they are weaker. Be harmonious, sympathetic, loving as brothers, compassionate, humble, and banish evil and vituperation from yourselves.

"He who wants to enjoy life must keep his tongue from speaking evil and uttering deceit. He must turn away from wrong and do right, and he must search for peace and keep it. God listens to the prayers of the righteous and is against those who practise evil.

"Revere Christ in your hearts and be ready to defend anyone who asks you in some way to show some of the hope that is in you. Maintain a clear conscience so that anyone who slanders you or accuses you falsely will be ashamed. Since Christ suffered physically, you must also arm yourselves with the same attitude, for he who has suffered physically has gained relief from sin, so that he now lives by what God wills.

"There should be no more indulging in unbridled lusts, in passions, in drinking parties, in carousing, in dissipations and forbidden idolatries, because you have to render account to God. Do everything by God and what He wills so that He may be glorified through Jesus Christ.

"Be happy that you are sharing to some degree the sufferings of Christ so that you will be full of joy when He reveals His Glory. Entrust your souls to God, do what is right, and love one another and God.

"The elders should set a good example to their congregations, and the younger men should show respect and humility to the elders. Exercise self-control, be on your guard against the devil, resist him, and know that throughout the world people are suffering. God will always re-establish you and lift you up. Peace."

THE SECOND GENERAL
EPISTLE OF PETER

This is a second epistle written by Peter the apostle.
"Grace and peace to you, through the knowledge of God
and Jesus our Lord. Supplement your faith with virtue, your
virtue with knowledge, your knowledge with self-control,
your self-control with patience, your patience with piety,
your piety with brotherly affection, and your brotherly affection with love. With these qualities, you will have knowledge of Jesus, you will never stumble, and you will enter the
Kingdom of God.

"I will shortly leave my human body, so I want to make
sure you keep these things in mind before I go. We actually
saw Jesus, so we are not making up stories for you. He is
truly the Son of God.

"Try to stay away from false prophets with their cleverly
devised plans to deceive and exploit you. If God can destroy
Sodom and Gomorrah, if He can flood the world and save
Noah, if He can rescue Lot from the immoral behaviour
of the lawless, then He is capable of anything, and He will
know how to rescue the Godless from temptation and keep
the wicked under punishment for the Day of Judgement.

"Those who yield to fleshly desires, indulge in polluting
passions, and despise authority will be punished. If one is
righteous and then strays to become wicked, then the last
condition becomes worse than the first.

"In the last days, people will scoff and behave immorally,
asking about the so-called promised Coming. They don't
know that the world was there before them and the heavens
are waiting to destroy them as soon as God gives the order.

"With God, one day is a thousand years, and a thousand
years is one day. God is patient, waiting for more people to

repent before He strikes! So try to be at peace with Him so that He will find you spotless and blameless.

"Regard God's continued patience as a chance for your salvation. Be on your guard so that you are not swayed away and lose your own stability. Grow in the Grace and knowledge of our Lord and Saviour Jesus Christ, to Whom be the Glory forever."

THE FIRST GENERAL EPISTLE OF JOHN

Written by John the author of the fourth Gospel to warn readers against false teachers and exhort them to hold fast to the Christian faith and fulfil all the Christian duties, especially love.

"We are writing about the Word of Life. We have seen Him, and the Life has been revealed to us, the eternal Life that existed with the Father. We want you also to enjoy our fellowship. God is the Light. If we walk in the Light, as He Himself is the Light, then we will enjoy fellowship with one another, and the Blood of His Son Jesus will cleanse us from all our sins. If we confess our sins, He will cleanse us, but if we say we have no sin, then we make Him out to be a liar, and His Word will not be in us.

"I write these things so that you may not sin, but if you do then Jesus is an atoning sacrifice for the sins of the whole world. If you love your brother, then you will remain in the Light. He who loves the world does not love the Father, but he who does the Will of God remains forever.

"The antichrist is coming. They are the ones who deny Jesus and God. If you deny One, you deny the Other. People will come and try to mislead you, but I know that the anointing you have received from Him remains in you, and you don't need teaching from anyone. Remain in Him so that when He does come, you will not be afraid of Him.

"God has lavished a wealth of love on us; that is why we are called children of God. When He comes, we shall see Him as He really is. Whoever practises sin will never see or know Him. Those born of God cannot commit sin, which belongs to the devil who Jesus came to destroy.

"Love one another, be righteous, and you will stay with God. Love in deeds and truth and not in word and tongue.

God knows everything and will know what is really in our hearts. He has told us to put our faith in Jesus Christ and to love one another, then whatever we ask Him, He will give to us.

"Don't believe every spirit but always put them to the test to see whether they are from God or not. Those not from God are spirits of the antichrist.

"God is love and whoever does not love does not know God. God loves us, that is why He sent His only begotten Son into the world to die for us so that through Him, we might live. He sent His Son as an atoning sacrifice for our sins. No one has ever seen God, but He loves us, so we should also love each other. He remains in us, and His love has been perfected in us. We know what love is because He first loved us. Anyone who loves God should also love his brother. True love of God means you must also obey His Commandments.

"Anyone born of God conquers the world, and faith is the victory that triumphs over the world. God's testimony through Jesus is stronger than everything and has granted us eternal life, which is the confidence we have in Him. Once you know that He is there, then He will grant you anything you ask of Him.

"All sins are bad, but there are some that end in death. Even though most of the world is dominated by the wicked, just remember that we belong to God, who has shown us how to know Him, and nothing can subdue us. We are in union with Jesus and God, so keep away from worshipping idols."

THE SECOND EPISTLE OF JOHN

The second epistle of John was written to exhort readers to hold fast to the Commandments they had received, to warn against false teachers who deny that Christ has come in the flesh (antichrist), and to tell them that He will soon visit them.

"We must all try to love one another, which means we have to obey His Commandments. Beware of imposters who don't believe that Christ was incarnated. They are all deceivers. Look out for yourselves so that you don't lose everything that you have worked for. In this way, you will obtain your full reward.

"Whoever assumes leadership and does not remain in the teaching of Christ, does not have God. Don't welcome anyone into your house who does not bring Christ's teaching."

THE THIRD EPISTLE
OF JOHN

The third epistle of John is addressed to Gaius to commend him for his Christian life and his hospitality to the evangelists sent by John and to censure Diotrephes for his bad conduct.

"Since Diotrephes loves to be prominent and does not accept our authority, I shall call attention to his activities when I arrive. He uses insinuating language and expels from the church, those who willingly welcome the brothers. Do not imitate evil but good. The well doer is from God, and the evil doer has no vision of God. Demetrius enjoys a good reputation from everyone and from truth itself. I will see you shortly. Peace to you and remember me to your friends."

THE GENERAL EPISTLE
OF JUDE

This epistle was written by Jude, a slave of Jesus and a brother of James.

"Certain people have sneaked in, impious ones who pervert the Grace of God into lust and deny Jesus. I remind you that God, after rescuing the people from Egypt, still destroyed the unbelievers. Even angels who misbehaved were punished, likewise Sodom and Gomorrah who were immoral.

"God will judge everybody and convict the ungodly for all their impious activities and all the harsh words the godless sinners have spoken against Him.

"Pray to the Holy Spirit, keep yourselves in the Love of God, and wait for the Mercy of our Lord Jesus Christ to give us eternal life. Convince those who are in doubt and save others from the fire so that through Jesus Christ, God will find you faultless in the abounding joy of His Glory."

REVELATION

This is the only New Testament book that is exclusively prophetic in character. It was written (so tradition tells us) by John the apostle on the island of Patmos, where he was imprisoned for his faith. It was addressed to seven churches (in Ephesus, Smyrna, Pergamum, Thyatira, Sardis, Philadelphia, and Laodicea) of the Roman province of Asia. It was written to correct the evils in the churches and to prepare them for the events that were about to confront them. This is the revelation of Jesus Christ that God granted Him to show what was shortly to take place.

The communication was sent via an angel to John who heard a voice and saw seven golden lampstands. Among them was someone like a son of man dressed in a long robe and with a golden sash round his chest. He had white hair, eyes of fire, and feet of precious ore. He had seven stars in His right hand. He said He was the same Jesus who had been crucified and asked John to write down everything He was to tell him. The Lord's Message to the seven churches was . . .

"I know how you have changed and so you must repent and go back to the way you were, or I will remove the lampstands from their place. Those who listen will be given the tree of life in God's Paradise. The devil will tempt you, but you must resist him and be faithful. Some of you are doing things against God even though you claim to belong to Him. You are practising idolatry and immorality and following the so-called prophetess Jezebel. I have given her time to repent, and if she does not, I will destroy her and her children.

"I will reward each person according to his works. Those who stick with Me will be given authority over all the nations. No one knows when I will come, so repent."

John then saw a throne with One (God) sitting on it in Heaven, looking like a precious stone surrounded by a rainbow. Surrounding the throne were twenty-four thrones with twenty-four elders dressed in white sitting on them. Seven torches (the seven Spirits of God) were burning around the throne. Four living beings, one like a lion, one like an ox, one like a man, and one like an eagle were also around the throne. They all had wings and were praising God. The other twenty-four elders were bowing down and worshipping God.

A Lamb (representing Jesus) was sacrificed, and he was the only One amongst the elders who could open God's scroll, and they sang songs praising Him, as He was worthy of the power, wealth, wisdom, strength, honour, glory, and blessing He had received from God because He was the One who had shed His Blood. The Lamb then opened seven seals, each of them depicting what was to happen to the world.

Some people would kill each other. Others would die by earthquake, plague, and wild beasts. The fifth seal was opened, and John was shown the souls of the dead who were pleading with God to spare them. They were given white robes and told to wait until all the killing was completed. The sixth seal revealed earthquakes, violent winds, stars falling out of the sky, and dislodged mountains. All the rich and powerful were hiding in caves cowering with fear from God. Then John saw four angels calm the elements and count those who were to be saved. They all wore white robes and worshipped and praised God with the elders, the angels, and the four living beings.

When the Lamb opened the seventh seal, John saw seven angels who each blew a trumpet, at the end of which were fire, hailstone, volcanoes, storms, locusts, scorpions, and other catastrophes that killed many people. The moon and sun became dark, and stars fell out of the sky.

All those who did not have God's seal of approval were tortured for five months by the scorpions, but refused the relief of death. After that, a third of mankind was destroyed by angels sent by God. The rest of mankind who escaped death, however, still did not repent nor forego their idolatries and immorality.

John was then told to eat a scroll from an angel. The scroll tasted sweet but had bitter and painful after effects on the stomach.

God will leave two olive trees and two lamps as witnesses. They will even have the power to stop rain, bring about all kinds of plagues, and turn water into blood. Anyone who injures them will be killed. After their testimonies, the trees and lamps will be killed by a beast, and their dead bodies left in the streets for three and a half days where people will be forced to look at them in places spiritually likened to Sodom and Egypt. After three and a half days, God will make them rise again, putting fear into all who saw it. They will then be made to rise up into the clouds.

Every hour after that, an earthquake will kill many people. The survivors will be so afraid they will be forced to believe in God. Then John saw all the elders worshipping God. His Temple was opened, and the Ark of His Covenant was seen in His Sanctuary followed by lightning, thunder, hail, and earthquakes.

A pregnant woman wearing a crown of twelve stars appeared and then a gigantic dragon (Satan) with seven heads, ten horns, and seven diadems on his heads also appeared. It tried to attack the woman, but she was saved by God who snatched her child to safety. There was a war in Heaven with Michael and his angels battling against the dragons and his angels, who were defeated and forced out of Heaven to the earth. Satan failed against the woman and Heaven and decided to fight against God's people on earth.

The dragon was given tremendous power on earth for forty-two months to blaspheme, steal, kill, confuse, and do everything else against God. He made sure he got many followers on earth who were impressed by his power. The Lamb then stood on Mount Zion with only 144,000 followers who had not gone against God.

Three angels came to warn people that whoever followed the dragon would die because the time had come for God to destroy them. The angels then swung their scythes, which signalled the destruction of the sinners.

All sea creatures perished when the angels began pouring the seven bowls of God's anger on earth. Rivers became blood, people died of ulcers, heat, darkness, pain in their bodies, and dehydration as the Euphrates dried up, and finally by thunder, lightning, earthquakes, and volcanoes.

John was shown a woman seated on a scarlet beast that had seven heads and ten horns. She was holding a gold cup containing all the abominations and impurities of her immorality. The horns and the heads represented future kings who would fight against the Lamb but would be destroyed. The woman is a harlot who will be hated and despised forever. The kings and those who committed fornication with her will also suffer. The angels, the elders, and four living beings all worshipped God for judging the harlot and imposing His Power on the world.

One must always worship God because Jesus' Testimony is the Spirit of prophecy.

A white horse representing The Word of God then destroyed the beast and all the sinners on earth by throwing them into an all-consuming fire of sulphur. Their flesh was eaten by birds. The dragon, the serpent, and Satan himself were locked up for a thousand years.

Those who followed God and suffered for Jesus came to life and reigned with Christ for a thousand years. The rest of the dead did not come to life until the thousand years were completed. Satan was released and finally destroyed in the fire.

Another scroll was opened that contained the Book of Life, and everybody was judged according to what he or she did. Anyone who was not recorded in the Book of Life was thrown into a lake of fire.

A new Heaven and earth emerged free from all sinners. There was a new Jerusalem. There was no sea, no sun, no moon, no night, no death, and no more suffering. God then said, "*It is done! I am the Alpha and the Omega*." No sinner will ever live in the new order, except those chosen by God.

John was then told by the angel that everything he had seen would come true. Those who were sinning should continue if they wanted, but God would come one day and destroy them all.

Jesus then said that He sent the angel to him in order for him to witness everything for the churches. No one should add or take away from this Book or God will destroy him.

The Grace of the Lord Jesus Christ be with everybody. Amen.

Lightning Source UK Ltd.
Milton Keynes UK
UKHW012137191121
394209UK00001B/129